DANCING WITH YOUR
LB 2395 G43 19

P9-DVH-757

DATE DUE

HOW TO STUDY—THE ZEN WAY

Relax. Prepare yourself to go on a journey to a place you've never been. Forget about the destination. Concentrate on the trip itself. Settle into what you are doing. Absorb and be absorbed by the task at hand. Embrace your books and dance.

The Zen approach has been applied to such diverse activities as poetry, archery, tea preparation and drinking, sword fighting, meditation, and motorcycle maintenance. Following the time-tested insights of Zen Buddhism, the method is disarmingly simple: Immerse yourself in each moment completely. Erase the line between performer and performance.

In a state of Zen mindfulness, the dancer becomes one with the dance. So, too, will this unique blending of Zen philosophy and effective study skills enable the student to stop wrestling with his or her books and dance. . . .

DANCING WITH YOUR BOOKS

J. J. GIBBS is a professor in the department of criminology at Indiana University in Indiana, Pennsylvania. He has an M.B.A. and a Ph.D. from the State University of New York at Albany. His work has appeared in numerous professional publications; *Dancing with Your Books* is his first book for a general audience.

DANCING WITH YOUR BOOKS

The Zen Way of Studying

J. J. GIBBS

A PLUME BOOK

PLUME
Published by the Penguin Group
Penguin Books USA Inc., 375 Hudson Street,
New York, New York 10014, U.S.A.
Penguin Books Ltd, 27 Wrights Lane,
London W8 5TZ, England
Penguin Books Australia Ltd, Ringwood,
Victoria, Australia
Penguin Books Canada Ltd, 10 Alcorn Avenue,
Toronto, Ontario, Canada M4V 3B2
Penguin Books (N.Z.) Ltd, 182-190 Wairau Road,
Auckland 10, New Zealand

Penguin Books Ltd, Registered Offices:
Harmondsworth, Middlesex, England

First published by Plume, an imprint of New American Library,
a division of Penguin Books USA Inc.
Published simultaneously in Canada.

First Printing, September, 1990
10 9 8 7 6 5 4

 REGISTERED TRADEMARK—MARCA REGISTRADA

Library of Congress Cataloging-in-Publication Data

Gibbs, John J.
    Dancing with your books : the Zen way of studying / by J.J. Gibbs.
      p.   cm.
    Includes bibliographical references.
    ISBN 0-452-26496-0
    1. Study, Method of.   I. Title.
LB1049.G53   1990
371.3′028′1—dc20   90-36517
                                                  CIP

Printed in the United States of America
Designed by Leonard Telesca

BOOKS ARE AVAILABLE AT QUANTITY DISCOUNTS WHEN USED TO PROMOTE PROD-
UCTS OR SERVICES. FOR INFORMATION PLEASE WRITE TO PREMIUM MARKETING
DIVISION, PENGUIN BOOKS USA INC., 375 HUDSON STREET, NEW YORK, NEW YORK
10014.

For John L. Gibbs, my father,
who taught me to keep my eye on the ball

and

For Mary R. O'Connor Gibbs, my mother,
who taught me to laugh when I missed it

Acknowledgments

This book started life as a Zen approach to statistical reasoning. Anne Campbell and Steven Muncer deserve recognition for pointing out that there are broader and more interesting applications of Zen to learning than to just statistics.

In its adolescence, the book grew into an overweight, awkward, and boring treatise. Robert Stricker, my agent, saw some potential where others had not, made some very insightful suggestions, and had the gumption to take on the project.

The book developed into maturity under the care of Gary Luke, my editor. I thank Gary for his suggestions and encouragement.

Thanks go to Nan Wizer, my friend, for her illustrations, and to all the other members of our little sangha in Indiana, PA, for their support and zillions of dharma yuks.

Finally, I would like to thank Kate Hanrahan, my wife, for her love, faith, and understanding, and our children, Sarah and Roddy Gibbs, for the way they make my heart sing.

CONTENTS

Part One

A NEW APPLICATION OF AN OLD PERSPECTIVE

Purpose of the Journey

I've been teaching college students for twenty years. For most of that time, I've been asking myself the same question: How can I make learning more fun and interesting for my students? After twenty years of trying different strategies and techniques, I've come to the conclusion that I've been posing the wrong question. It's a foolish but common mistake.

Before inquiring about how to make studying and learning more fun, I should have searched for reasons why it isn't fun. Indeed, many people feel it is downright painful.

Schoolwork is painful for many college students because they don't know how to get out of their own way. This is the main concern of this book. I'll show you how to deal with all the things that students do to make learning harder than it has to be.

Although much of the advice contained in this book was written with college students in mind, the principles presented can be applied to any learning situation. It doesn't matter what you are trying to learn—automotive repair, the harmonica, modern dance, or akido—or who is teaching you—friend, professor, mentor, or yourself. The approach presented in this book will help you.

The premise of this book is that learning does not have to be a chore. Much of the pain, anguish, and discomfort associated with schoolwork is unnecessary and avoidable.

Each day of studying, of course, is not a new experience in pain. Most students experience the thrill of learning and the joy of performing well at some point in their academic careers. Everybody likes to learn something interesting and useful. Everyone feels pride and happiness when they receive a good grade in a tough course. It is the process of learning and succeeding that most students find burdensome. Hitting the books, cramming for exams, and grinding out papers are hardly phrases that spawn images of young scholars lost in the ecstasy of a labor of love.

Most people I know value the results of learning and receiving recognition for learning well. However, they have a much less sanguine view of the process of learning. Studying, writing, completing assignments, and attending classes and labs are often considered painful necessities. The point this book makes is that they do not have to be.

The thrust of the book is that the process of learning not only can be just as enjoyable as the results, but also it makes good sense to focus more on process than on results. Studying does not have to be a battle with your books. It can be more like a dance with your books. If you faithfully follow the prescriptions that follow, you can learn that dance. Of course, as every dancer knows, attaining proficiency is demanding work that requires patience, flexibility, persistence, and endurance.

The first and most important step in learning to dance with your books is to get out of your own way. This means you must learn to focus on the dance itself. If you pay too much attention to how you look while you are dancing, how much effort the dance takes, or how much recognition you will receive for dancing well, it takes away from the dance. Learning to dance with your books—or doing anything else right—requires that you become less self-centered and more task-centered, or less self-conscious and more conscious of the task at hand, in your case, studying.

Stated in its most radical and seemingly paradoxical form, the central proposition of this book is that the less the self is consciously present in the performance of schoolwork, or any other work, the more of the self there is available to do the work. In other words, thinking about yourself gets in the way of what you are trying to do. Although it sounds bizarre, I think the biggest problem most students face is getting out of their own way so their natural intelligence can do the work it is supposed to do unencumbered.

The idea that the right approach to doing anything is to focus on the task rather than yourself is hardly novel. Expanding awareness or consciousness of the world by paying less attention to yourself and more attention to daily activities is part of many philosophies of life that stress the importance of the present. Zen, the approach to life on which this book is based, places a great deal of emphasis on the task at hand and the present moment.

You may wonder how Zen, a perspective that is commonly associated with mysticism, can possibly have anything to do with your day-to-day, here-and-now, down-to-earth struggle with the books. Many practitioners of Zen object to the mystical label because it implies that Zen has nothing to do with the everyday world of washing socks, making lunch, and grinding out a term paper. Zen has everything to do with these activities. It *is* these activities. Those who practice Zen point out that Zen is a very practical and rational approach to life and is anything but otherworldly. You will see as you read this book that Zen is exclusively focused on this life. Its central concern is the quality of life as expressed in everyday events and activities. Since school work qualifies as a common activity, Zen applies.

Zen has had a great influence on Japanese culture, and it has been applied to or expressed through a diversity of activities in Japan—for example, poetry, archery, tea preparation and drinking, painting, calligraphy, flower arranging, karate, judo, akido, kendo, and rock gardening. In the contemporary West, Zen has been suggested as an approach to many activities—psychoanalysis, organizational management, social work, running, cross-country skiing, and driving a car. Why not studying?

I am convinced that if you incorporate the suggestions in this book into your life and faithfully follow them, your academic work will eventually become less burdensome and more satisfying. I am also convinced that you will become more effective not only in your academic pursuits but also in other areas of your life. The principles I will describe have broad applicability, and they have been tested in the fires of experience. Zen masters would have it no other way.

What Is Zen?

Zen has been described as the art of living. According to the Zen masters, life as art or living right requires that we pay full attention to whatever we are doing at the moment. Life can be lived only in the present, and the task to be performed in the present should demand our full attention. Inattention is, to the Zen master, the most serious mistake. The ideal life is one of "perfect momentariness" in which we are fully involved in each moment.

Zen deals with the relationship of the self to the world, a part of which is the relationship of self to the task at hand. The perfect relationship is one in which there is no separation between the person and the task. There is no person and there is no task. There is only the doing of the task in the moment. It is similar to the way some dancers describe perfect dancing as the dancer and the dance becoming one. There is no subject-object or person-task duality. There is no dancer doing a dance. At the point at which the dancer and the dance meet—the present—there is only dancing, the activity. The purpose of Zen is to create such moments in everyday life by focusing attention on the activity of the present. The Zen prescription for living life to the fullest is to become absorbed in the task at hand.

This book is concerned with only one task—learning.

The main point of the book is that your relationship to your books should be much like the relationship between the dancer and the dance. You can be one. There is no need to bear down, to conquer the material in your books, or to resist the temptation to do anything but your schoolwork. All you have to do is remove, not overcome, the impediments that separate you from your studying. The way to do this is simply learn to do what you have to do in the moment, and realize you are what you do in that moment. You and your books are like the dancer and the dance. Embrace your books, and dance.

You Are Already the Perfect Student

A basic premise of Zen is that we are already enlightened. In other words, we all have the ability to see things as they really are, to live in the moment, and achieve full awareness. We all possess the spiritual gear needed to reach realization. All that remains is to put this gear into operation. We must remove the rust and years of accumulated gunk that keep our spiritual wheels from turning.

The job of the Zen master is to help us discover the best method for cleaning our gear. Put another way, he is there to show us the way by which we can clear the obstructions and break the attachments that blind us from seeing the truth. He does not advise us to add anything new to ourselves. He does not suggest that we build character or add new dimensions to our personality. He simply recommends that we remove the impediments to realizing our own true nature. He wants us to see ourselves as we really are and to become ourselves.

A basic premise on which this book is based is that every student has the ability to learn. The intelligence to learn and perform well in school already exists within you. In order to learn, you need only have faith that the ability is there; all that remains is its realization. In many cases, there will be impediments that must be removed before the realization of ability and understanding can take place. This book offers an approach to pushing aside the barriers to understanding. The purpose of this book is to help you to release the student within.

The methods presented in this book are intended to help each student work up to his or her potential. Obviously, potential varies by natural ability and previous effort and training. Intellectual capacity, for example, ranges from half-pints to gallons, to use Mortimer Adler's analogy. No claim is made that the approach to learning presented can turn half-pints into Nobel laureates. The approach can, however, help every student perform well in school. More important, the approach can help each student make the time spent on school work a rich and meaningful experience, regardless of his or her intellectual capacity.

Once you develop the ability to study with full concentration you will see for yourself what an enriching experience it is. Until then, I hope anecdotal accounts of the experience of enhanced awareness and recent psychological research on "flow states" and "mindfulness" will convince you of the possibility and benefits of studying with full concentration.

Research on flow states, which includes studying people during peak performance, has been conducted at the University of Chicago by Mihaly Csikszentmihalyi for more than ten years. Flow is a state of effortless effort that results from being totally absorbed in an activity. It is what athletes call being in the zone. When in flow or in the zone, all your faculties are working in perfect harmony to accomplish a single task. There are no wasted motions. There are no irrelevant thoughts. Attention is completely focused. You experience a heightened sense of awareness. You feel more alive than ever before. Everything is as it should be. You just go with the flow.

Sound pretty good? It is. Sound like something you will never achieve, especially while studying? It isn't. You have probably been in this state at one point in your life, and you can learn techniques that will help you get into flow.

Mindfulness, which has been studied by Harvard psychologist Ellen Langer and her colleagues, is a state of active attention. In a series of experiments, Langer used fairly simple techniques to train people to be more mindful or, as Langer describes it, "to see the moment more creatively by paying more attention." She found that mindfulness influences health and longevity, that mindfulness or active attention, as opposed to strained concentration, not only enhances life but also can actually extend it.

Everyone has the potential to enter a state of mindfulness or flow. It is natural. All that is needed is to remove the impediments that restrict our natural flow. We have to open the dam walls that have been built by years of strained attention and self-absorption in order to reestablish our natural flow.

Some of the techniques presented and advice offered in this book to increase flow or mindfulness are twenty-five hundred years old. They are simple practices that have withstood the test of time. Taken together, they are the art of living. When applied to learning, they are the art of studying or dancing with your books.

Rules of the Road

Much of the literature on self-knowledge and self-awareness is devoted to description, discussion, and exploration of what has variously been termed the path, journey, way, or road to enlightenment. A great deal of what has been written about the path to becoming fully conscious, the art of life, is applicable to learning to dance with your books, the art of studying.

There are only two rules of the road—take the first step, and continue walking. The time to start is now. Don't wait until you feel just right, lose ten pounds, get over your cold, mend your broken heart, or quit smoking. We are all familiar with waiting for that "something" that will settle everything so we can get on with the "important things." However, we all know that either that "something" never comes, or when it does its tenure is brief, and we await that "something else" that will make everything right in our lives.

Don't wait. There is no perfect moment in the offing. There is only one right moment—the present moment. Don't waste your time waiting for the time that is just right. Don't live in the expectation that there will be some future moment when your real life will begin and everything will be free and easy. Put your unsteady foot on the path. Take that first step, with all your problems and misgivings. Keep walking. Walk on when you're tired. Walk on when you're mad. Walk on when you're happy. Walk on when you would rather be sailing, bowling, fishing, partying, power shopping, iron pumping, or whale watching.

Right now is the time to make the commitment to learn to study right, that is, to study with full attention. Once the commitment is made you must put your intention into action by trying to study with full attention each time you study, which should be often. The desire to study right is not enough. Thinking and reading about studying right are not enough. You must practice studying right each time you study. And you must study despite boredom, a broken heart, an aching head.

Although the one and only right way to study, or do anything else, is with full attention, there are many ways to study right. Each person must find the approach that best suits him. The principles and methods suggested in this book are general. They merely point the way to the path. They are not the path itself. Each individual is responsible for finding his own path by adapting the principles and methods presented to his personal style.

Much of what will be presented in this book may appear to some as little more than simple ideas that are charming to the intellect and may strike others as downright trite folk sayings. Both views are rooted in the same soil—words. Words have to be used to convey ideas. But ideas have to be put into practice to be valuable. The value is in the experience. The suggestions made in this book are meant to be more than intellectually satisfying or intellectually grating. Put them into practice if you want to derive any benefit.

Ideas like "live fully in the moment" and "do only what you are doing" sound trite. They are platitudes that are responded to with sighs and jeers. They are hackneyed phrases that provoke cynicism and sarcasm. The effects of putting these ideas into practice, however, are anything but trite. When the principles that are locked in these bromides are realized in action, they have tremendous implications.

It is easy to understand intellectually the principles that are presented in this book. Their realization, a deep understanding that comes from personal experience, is another matter. It requires great patience and effort.

The last rule of the road before the journey begins is that you should not mistake what is written in this book for Zen practice. Of course, part of Zen practice is to do everything you do with full awareness, so the book does promote Zen practice in a limited application to studying. But Zen encompasses much more of life. Indeed, Zen is life as it really is. The concepts and techniques presented in this book are merely borrowed from the Zen literature and applied to schoolwork.

Lay of the Land

This book is divided into five parts. The first part, "New Application of an Old Perspective," is devoted to the discussion of Zen principles and their broad application to schoolwork. The main purpose of this part of the book is to convince you that developing a new attitude, called right effort, toward your work will result in a more meaningful and productive educational experience. The emphasis of the introductory part of the book is on demonstrating that some cherished values and beliefs, for example, strong future orientation and self-focus, can be impediments to performance. Try to keep an open mind while reading this part of the book. It isn't easy to accept ideas that run counter to conventional notions about work and school that are so familiar and well entrenched that we think we were born with them in our brains.

The second part of the book, "Clearing and Calming the Mind," provides instructions for attaining the state of mind conducive to studying with right effort. This part of the book is concerned with the purpose and method of one kind of meditation, zazen, or zen sitting. Meditation is a way to develop the ability to both concentrate and relax. In meditation, you achieve a state of relaxed alertness that, when applied to school-work, translates into long periods of effective studying.

The third part of the book, "Maintaining Quality and Enthusiasm," draws heavily from Robert Pirsig's *Zen and the Art of Motorcycle Maintenance*. Part Three describes gumption traps, or problems, that can interfere with the application of right effort to your studies, and it discusses techniques and methods for dealing with these problems. Select the techniques and methods that work for you. Feel free to modify techniques. Tailor them to your particular problems and style.

The fourth part of the book discusses the skills you need to perform well in school, such as reading, writing, and listening. The approaches presented are to be considered suggestions. There are plenty of books about study skills. If those offered in this book do not suit you, go to other sources.

The final part of the book contains a review of important ideas and techniques. It also features a description of several books on Zen for those who want to do further reading.

A great deal of practical information is presented in this book. *Practical* means that what is written is intended to be put into practice. Its value can only be realized in practice. Just knowing what is in this book is of little value to you. The simple and obvious point is that you have to apply what you read to your studies; in most cases, it will take more than one try to get it right. It will take constant practice to keep it right.

This book is intended to be used as a reference book. The suggested way to read this book is first to read it from cover to cover to see if the approach makes sense to you. If it does, commit yourself to a program of study with right effort, and begin putting the concepts and techniques presented in the book into practice in your life. Before you put specific techniques into practice, reread the sections describing those techniques. Every now and then, reread the entire book. There could be useful information that you have not put into practice because you have forgotten it. Reread also because the information will be much more valuable and interesting after you have tried to incorporate it into your daily life.

The Tyranny of Time

A central component of many problems faced by students and others is the management of time. When you consider the central place that time holds in our lives, it isn't any wonder that it can present difficulties for many. Time is a valuable commodity. Often we cannot get enough of it. It is a currency. We spend it. We invest it. We worry about wasting it.

Time is motion. It often passes too quickly. Time flies. It passes us by. Or time passes too slowly. It drags. Sometimes we spend our time wondering how to pass the time. But no matter how we spend our time, time marches on. It keeps ticking along second by second, minute by minute. It cannot be stopped.

Time is the way we mark our lives. Yesterday, today, tomorrow ... A little while ago ... When I was little ... When I grow up ... The good old days ... The bad old days ... When my ship comes in.

Time is place. Here is now, the present. There is past or future. At some point in time, our time is up, and we enter a different kind of time or no time at all.

Time is the ruler of modern life. Entire industries

have been built around saving time—time management consultants, for example, and all kinds of convenience goods. It seems that time has enslaved us. We never have enough of it. We have too much to do in too little time. This can result in a problem of time-place dissonance. It is a problem that can affect how effectively and comfortably you study.

The time-place dissonance problem can be seen as one of trying to be in two places at one time or two times in one place. Sometimes when we are pressed for time, we are thinking of what we have to do next—the future—or what we have just finished doing—the past—while we are doing something in the present.

When you were reading the last section, were you thinking only of what you were reading? Or were you thinking about what you could be doing instead of reading? Or what you were doing before you were reading? Or what you would do after you finished reading? If you were thinking about anything other than what you were reading, you were in a state of time-place dissonance, and you were not concentrating wholly on what you were supposed to be doing. In other words, your energy was divided between the present and some other time.

The Zen solution to time-place dissonance, and all other problems related to time, like anxiety and worry, is simple: Do only what you are doing in the present. The aim of this book is to help you do only what you are doing through techniques designed to keep you in the present moment.

Be Where You Are

Every September, my wife, Kate, gives me a new coffee cup to start the new school year. The message printed on this year's cup reads,

THOUGHT FOR TODAY:
NO MATTER WHERE YOU GO,
THERE YOU ARE.

This is one of my favorite cups. Not only because most people think the caption is at least mildly amusing, but also because it is so simply true. The saying on the cup is a reminder to me to keep my mind on what I am doing in the present. It helps me be where I am, which is the only place I actually can be.

At this very moment, if you are reading this book, you cannot be anywhere else. There is only this place, this activity, and this moment. You cannot actually be in the past or the future, so you cannot be in another place doing something else, although you can think about it. You can only be in the present. You can only exist now.

To be fully engaged in the moment, you must give your full attention to what you are doing at the moment. If you are reading this book, read this book. If you are thinking about the great time you had last night, the gang of laundry you have to do tonight, or how you will outlaw English grammar when you are master of the universe, you are not fully involved in the task at hand.

When you sit down to study or sit in a class, *be there*! You can't be anyplace else, anyway. Of course, you can get up and go do something else, but by the time you do this, it is a different moment. At the very moment you are studying or in class, it is futile to think that you can be somewhere else. It only causes problems, and takes your mind away from what you should be studying.

When you sit down to study or sit in class, accept that you will have to be there for an hour or more, and concentrate on what you are doing. As long as you have to be there, *be there*. There is no place else you can be.

Living fully requires that you do only what you are doing while you are doing it. When you are studying, do not think of anything except what you are studying. Don't even think about how happy and proud you will be when you learn this lesson or many lessons. Concentrate totally on this lesson. Now! Don't just go through the motions. The time to learn is not in the future. The time to learn is now.

The idea that you can only be where you are is easily grasped intellectually by most people. As a practical matter, however, putting the idea into operation is not so easy. It takes patience and practice.

Staying Centered in the Moment

Existing fully in the here and now, or attaining time-place consonance, requires staying centered in the moment. You cannot let other times and places pull you away from the present. What you are doing should remain solidly in the center of your life. Everything else should remain on the periphery, far from the center.

Most of us live lives that are a whirlwind of activities, aspirations, fantasies, worries, regrets, triumphs, desires, disappointments, responsibilities, and competing demands. At any time, the cyclone of thoughts and emotions can sweep us away. The virulent winds of emotion and spinning storm of thoughts of the past and future, however, remain calm in the center of the cyclone, which represents the present.

The eye of the storm, or center, is a place of calmness, clarity, and unity. There is only one center, just as there is only one present. As one moves from the center toward the circumference of the spiraling circles of the storm, an increasing number of points can be located; just as one's thoughts move from the present to the past and future, there are an increasing number of points in time. There is only one present. It is the moment you are in now. There are many pasts and futures. And the cumulative number of past and future events available to occupy your mind increases as you move farther away from the present.

Staying centered means that all your energy and attention are concentrated on the task, problem, or activity at hand. This does not mean, of course, that the future and the past are not relevant to our lives.

What we are doing in the present should be informed by the past and future. Our past experiences shape what we do, how we do it, and why we do it. If an approach you took to writing a research paper or taking an exam was unsuccessful a number of times in the past, you should take another tack the next time you are faced with the same task.

Our future goals, objectives, aspirations, and dreams also affect what we do in the present. The direction we want to go in our lives is the criterion by which we make some choices. If you want to be a mathematician, you should not major in modern literature. But you should take courses in modern literature, just because you are interested in it or you want to round out your education.

The point is we should not forget about the past and future. The past and future inform the present. It is important to keep in mind, however, that they are not the present. We must not let them intrude too much on the present. They are background. They provide a broad framework for our lives, but they should not interfere with present activities. If you want to be a geologist but all the time you are studying geology you are fantasizing about how irresistibly attractive you will be to the opposite sex once you get your degree and become a rock star, you will not learn much geology.

Being centered in the moment and focused on the task at hand does not mean that there is no room in your life for flashes of insight into your past, visions of the future, or epiphanies that manifest solutions to problems that have been on your mind. The danger lies in getting stuck in unproductive or counterproductive thoughts about the future or past as the present moment passes by.

There undoubtedly will be times when the task at hand will be to review the past or plan for the future. These are, however, activities that are done in the present. You should make sure that you stay centered in the present while you do them. When you review, review. When you plan, plan. And keep your reviewing and planning within a restricted time frame. If you catch yourself fantasizing about the year 2525 when you are supposed to be planning for the paper that is due at the end of the semester, you are beyond the boundaries of the present. You are not centered.

Letting Go

Concentration is not a matter of gritting your teeth, furrowing your brow, and pushing hard. Thinking and studying should be natural. Our brains are original equipment. They fit in with the rest of us, and are built for easy use. Additional attachments and sophisticated gizmos are not needed to make our minds work for us. Nothing extra is need. All we have to do is let our brains do the work they were designed to do.

Active attention to the task at hand does not require that you strain your brain. When your concentration is right, it is effortless. Your mind just goes with the flow of mental activities required to understand the material you are studying.

There is some research evidence to support the observation that the full mental absorption characteristic of active attention does not tax the brain. Researchers at the National Institute of Mental Health discovered that the strained or effortful concentration required when people push themselves to work on an irrelevant or uninteresting task results in higher levels of cortical arousal than does the effortless concentration characteristic of the previously described "flow states." The differences in patterns of brain function associated with effortless and strained concentration suggest that the approach to studying proposed in this book actually requires less energy than the brain-busting or mind-over-matter approach to studying with which many of us have years of experience.

Concentrating on what you are doing at the moment is simply a matter of letting go of what you are not doing at the moment. In other words, you have to accept being where you are and doing what you are doing. You have to let go of everything else. All else, that is, other times and places, is not relevant to the task at hand. It takes your attention away from what you are doing.

You do not have to force other times and places, with attendant thoughts and feelings, from your mind. Just let them go. Allow your mind to concentrate its full power on what you are doing at the moment, for example, studying or writing.

The Zen approach is simple and economical. It is a bare-bones approach, with nothing extra added. Additional motivation, purpose and structure are not needed to concentrate. All that is needed is to empty the mind and leave it open to be filled with whatever needs to be done.

Awareness or mindfulness of the moment and what requires doing in the moment is a form of concentration. The mind must be relaxed and open to be aware. Thoughts, especially preconceptions and judgments, result in a closed mind and can impede concentration and learning. For example, if you enter a required course, say, statistics, with a closed mind, which is reflected in statements like "I hate statistics, only dweebs major in it" and "I hate statistics, I'll never understand it," your attention will be divided when you study, most likely unevenly, between the content of the course and how much you hate it. In order to concentrate fully on the content of the course, you have to let go of your hate, and other thoughts and feelings about the course, and open your mind to the material to be learned.

Learning requires a nimble, supple, and clear mind. Thoughts about anything other than the task at hand make for a murky, boggy mind. When the mind is attached or clings to thoughts and feelings that are not pertinent to the moment, it becomes sluggish, cluttered, and confused. It becomes tangled in the tendrils of unproductive thoughts and choking emotions. The moment is lost in the miasma.

At other times, the unfocused mind can race out of control. Overwhelmed by useless chatter and irrelevant clatter, it jumps from the present to the past and the future. Thoughts and emotions flash into consciousness incessantly. Each captures your attention for an instant. Happy. Friend. Last week's test ... Career. Mother. Pay the rent ... Do I have a future? Should I cut my hair? ... Love. Death. Socks and underwear. The clamoring of what the Zen masters call our monkey mind turns our attention away from the all-important moment.

Chinese Handcuffs

Clearing the murky mind stuck in errant thought and calming the racing mind careening from thought to thought require the same familiar strategy—letting go. Hard pulling, pushing, cutting, and blocking are not necessary. Indeed, such approaches get us even more involved in unnecessary thoughts and emotions. Such strategies are akin to pulling on Chinese handcuffs. The harder you pull, the more tightly they grip your fingers.

There is a Catch-22 involved in trying to deal directly and forcefully with thoughts and emotions that are interfering with concentration on studying or other schoolwork. Paying special attention to the intrusive thoughts and emotions makes them even more powerful obstructions, and we can become stuck in coping with being stuck instead of concentrating on schoolwork.

The Zen approach to unproductive thoughts and disquieting emotions is simply to recognize them for what they are and not let the mind abide in them. If you do not attach to them, they will pass naturally, without great disturbance to your concentration on the task of the moment. Just relax, and let them go. Do not make them into more than they are. They are nothing special.

When your mind wanders from your studies, and thoughts of other times, places, and topics enter your mind, do not pursue them or suppress them. Just acknowledge them and return to work. If some thought is persistently intrusive or you have a wonderful insight while studying, write it down, and return to it when you are finished studying.

Negative judgments and feelings will undoubtedly arise on your journey through school. At some time in our educational careers, we all feel bored, tired, angry, frustrated, confused, or depressed. The key to letting these feelings go and getting back to work is to treat them dispassionately. Do not associate them with yourself. Do not say, "I'm bored. This is hopeless. I'll never learn this stuff." Simply say, "Boredom is here." Merely acknowledge that boredom has arrived on the scene. Do not try to get away from it. Do not get stuck in it. Let it go, and continue to do what you are doing in the moment.

Consider the arrival of boredom an indication that you are not in the moment. If you were, there would be no boredom, anxiety, or any other emotion that results from thinking about a future state. Boredom means that you are not satisfied with where you are and what you are doing. You want to be someplace else doing something else. Another place and activity by definition have to be in the future. If you are wholly in the present, that is, you accept the moment and concentrate exclusively on what you are doing, the future, and feelings associated with it like boredom and anxiety, will not be a concern.

Control and Freedom

Let go! Relax into life! Accept what is! Does all this sound pretty passive? Who's in control? Isn't getting some control over your life desirable? Of course it is. Dozens of studies demonstrate that a sense of control is important to quality of life. This is exactly what the Zen approach gives you. By accepting what you have to do, and letting go, you actually gain control and freedom.

Many of us are at the mercy of feelings and thoughts. They control our lives. If we are not feeling just right, we don't study or we study ineffectively. If thoughts about an old friend or lost pet cross our minds while we are working, we pursue them. If someone says unkind words to us, we cling to them, and they interfere with our work. If our motivation is low, we wait for it to emerge from some mysterious place in our psyche before we resume studying. Talk about being out of control!

Freedom means unrestrained action. It means to act in an uninhibited way. It does not mean that you blindly follow feelings, whims, or ephemeral desires. If you do, you are pushed or pulled by them. They shape your behavior. They are in control. You are not free.

The term *freedom,* as used here, means that you can react to the circumstances of the moment in an unrestrained way. You are in the driver's seat. You are in control. Irrelevant thoughts, desires, and emotions do not inhibit your behavior. They cannot drag you away or seduce you into doing anything other than what needs to be done in the moment.

Relax! Let go! Be free to dance with your books!

Relaxed Mind, Alert Mind

Relaxation does not mean that the mind goes to sleep. It means to let go to allow the mind to devote its full power to the task at hand. Emptying the mind or letting go is liberation from disquieting thoughts and feelings so our mind's light can shine directly and exclusively on the present moment, the task at hand. The remaining mind is relaxed but alert. It is taut and ready; poised to deal with whatever present circumstances demand.

The concentrated or empty mind is like a flame burning with great intensity. The flame burns brightly in pure oxygen. All gases that retard burning have been swept away. Only a clear blue flame remains. When you study, study as if there is a hard, clear, steady flame inside you illuminating the page, which contains the knowledge needed to keep the flame burning.

The Tyranny of Emotions

Soen-roshi, a modern Zen master, admonishes, "Do not be a slave to your moods and emotions. It is sunny, then it is cloudy; do not cling to either. Just march on!" John Daido Loori, an American Zen master, advises, "What we've got to learn to do, as we experience a feeling, is to make a notation, witness it. To witness means simply to be aware of it and then to go on, not to let this barrier we've created stop us from going any further." Such liberation from feelings and other disturbances is essential to proper concentration; a state that may be especially difficult to achieve when embarking on a new study regimen or program. From the beginning, it is important to disregard restrictive emotions and plunge into your studying with your whole mind. Do not wait for just the right moment, when your motivation and energy reach a peak, to begin. If you do, you will never get started.

There is even a method of personal therapy grounded in Zen principles that addresses the problem of getting started despite emotional resistance. In his book *Playing Ball on Running Water*, David Reynolds describes Morita therapy as an approach that considers life as a series of things to do and emphasizes action or getting things done. Feelings that sometimes emerge as unpleasant resistances to or consequences of accomplishing a necessary task should not be dwelled upon. They are simply accepted as part of doing what needs to be done and in this way relegated to a position where they do not have the power to obstruct.

Positive feelings or the emotional drive that some people think they need to get the job done are also deemphasized in the Morita approach. Action is dependent on only one thing: something needs to be done. This is an economical approach. There is nothing extra. In the Moritist method of personal management, once the value of a goal, for example, obtaining a degree or diploma, has been established, you simply do what needs to be done and accept whatever feelings arise. Remember, feelings come and go. What needs to be done remains until it is done.

Is There No Excitement or Joy?

Disregard feelings. Let them go. Take care of business. Just study. Do these words strike you as cold and flat? Does the Zen approach to studying mean that if your dog dies in front of your desk, you dispassionately remove the carcass and continue with your work? Are there no shrieks of eureka when your computer program finally works? Is there no celebration when you get an A on a test or a paper?

Of course there is joy in the Zen approach. Zen is a celebration of life. It is delighting in life as it is, moment by moment. Once you learn to handle disturbing thoughts and emotions and to concentrate on doing what needs to be done in the moment, your work will bring you great satisfaction. You will sometimes experience a sense that everything is all right. Everything seems to click. All is smooth. Easy. Skate City.

This state has been described by athletes. They play some games or matches in which everything seems easy and goes right. They are relaxed, but totally involved in the game. It is effortless.

Dancers try to achieve a similar state. They describe it as the dancer and the dance becoming one. Everything is done correctly, without effort. All is right. The rhythm. The steps. The music. There is unity. There is nothing but the dance.

Of course, achieving this state takes dedication and constant practice. It requires practicing and performing despite cold feet, pulled muscles, and fatigue. Above all, it requires that each dance is danced as if it were the last dance. The only dance that matters is the one performed in the present.

Even professional athletes, dancers, and musicians, who are dedicated to their sport or art, sometimes dread the drudgery of constant practice. They will invariably tell you that the hardest part is getting started. Other commitments, nagging injuries, questions of purpose, crises of confidence all come to mind: "Why do I do this?" "What's the use?" "I'll never be really good." "They'll probably find out some day that doing this shortens the life span." "I just don't feel like it today. I'll do a double session on Tuesday." "I guess I should polish all my shoes and clean the bathroom tiles with a toothbrush before I get started."

Once they get into the practice, and get fully involved in what they are doing, all the emotional resistances, which interfered with getting started, fall away. There is no question of why practice. No one is asking. There is only the crack of the bat when it meets the ball, the snap of punches returning after they hit the heavy bag, the feel of floor when the foot hits after a graceful leap, the touch of the tongue as the harmonica belts out a blues riff, the sound of the band when it's cookin'. Everything is all right. Everything is just right. Everything flows.

Just as athletes, dancers, and musicians must practice despite resistance, you must study despite initial misgivings. If you want to experience the joy of being immersed in your studies, you must study every day. And the more you do it, the better you will get at it.

Right Effort

We are all familiar with the old saying, "If you are going to do the job, do it right!" This is called right effort in Zen. It is doing your best at whatever life brings to you to be done. It is the single principle by which some men and women live their lives.

Right effort requires complete attention to the task at hand. All else is extra. There should be no thoughts of consequences or gain. There is only the effort in the moment. If you are thinking of what your effort in the moment will get you, you are not in the moment. There is only the doing. Nothing else exists.

Excessive thoughts of ambition, pride, and reward can destroy right effort. This may seem counterintuitive. Are these not the very things that motivate us to do things? Are not visions of Wall Street, Broadway, and Easy Street there to encourage us to keep our noses in the books and take our studies seriously? Don't we study or do anything else for a reason—to keep up, to get ahead, to go beyond? What about the carrot? The prize? Just deserts? To get a good job, get a good education. Be somebody. Study the classics and become well rounded without gaining weight.

There is nothing wrong with directing your efforts toward some desirable future state. However, when thoughts of the future interfere with concentration in the present, the trouble begins.

Right effort requires that you concentrate only on what you are doing in the moment. Thoughts of consequences are thoughts of the future, not of the present. They only get in the way. They take your attention away from what you are doing instead of bringing it into sharper focus. You have usually decided on the value of what you are about to do, for example, study for an exam or write a paper, long before you do it. If such activities were not of value to you in some way, you would not be enrolled in school. To think of the value or consequences of the act while you are acting is to add something extra. It takes away from the doing itself.

In operational terms, right effort means that if the score is 100 to 0 in the ninth inning and you're at bat with an 0 and 2 count, you still do the best you can. Not because it makes you look good—you're not a quitter. Not because there is always a chance of winning—win, lose, it doesn't matter. You put in one hundred percent every time you bat because when you're at bat, you bat. There is nothing but batting. If you are thinking about the hopelessness of the situation, how ridiculous the team looks, your wounded ego, or how good a cold drink is going to taste when the game is over, you are not batting one hundred percent. Even if you hit a home run, your effort is not right effort.

Here is the hardest part of right effort for most of us to accept: right effort is selfless or egoless effort. Ego is extra. If we are concerned with how we look or what something is going to do for us while we are doing our job, we are thinking of something other than what we are doing. It is the doing that counts, not what the doing will do for us. Thoughts of ego or self are assessments of how our actions will look in the eyes of some audience. Such thoughts take us out of the moment and into the future.

Studying with right effort requires that you become task-oriented rather than self-oriented. When effort is perfectly right, the self dissolves and only the task remains.

"Nonsense," you say. "I'm the one who does things for me. My purpose in going to school is to learn so I can make something of myself. How can I not think of myself? Why shouldn't I concentrate on me?" You may be going to school for all these reasons, but if they clutter your mind when you are studying, you are not studying with right effort. If you are thinking about what your effort is going to do for you while you're putting in the effort, you are thinking of your effort and the intended consequences of your effort, and, consequently, attention is divided between the present and the future.

Beginner's Mind

One way to promote right effort in your studies is to assume the attitude that is known as "beginner's mind" in the Zen literature. Beginner's mind is an empty mind. It is to approach each situation or task without expectations or preconceptions. It is a willingness to accept what happens, to deal with life as it unfolds.

Beginner's mind is a perspective that is always fresh. It is the realization that no matter how many times a task or situation has been encountered, it is always new, each time is different, and it warrants complete concentration and sincere effort. Beginner's mind is present mind. It recognizes that the situation or task at hand is a unique event that only occurs in the present moment. Beginner's mind knows that what life brings to be done in each moment is a new beginning, a whole world unto itself that will never appear again.

Beginner's mind is more than just acquiring a perspective that makes all situations *seem* new and exciting, it *is* seeing the world as it is in all this subtlety and complexity. The beginner's mind is wholly absorbed in the situation and allows the circumstances, which are constantly changing, to dictate the action. The beginner's mind pays active attention to the situation and recognizes that the flow of events in life makes each situation different.

Applied to studying, beginner's mind means recognizing that each reading, writing, or problem-solving session is unique. In other words, each task must be approached as if it is being done for the first time, no matter how many times it has been done before.

Actually, each time something is done, for example, writing or studying, it is the first time, because the circumstances and specifics of the task vary in ways that range from subtle to obvious each time the task is done. If we do not give the task our complete attention, as a beginner would, we might miss that little or big something that is essential to doing the job right. For example, for the good baseball player there are no routine plays. Each play and each aspect of its execution require complete involvement. A minuscule lapse in concentration can mean a major error.

Although there are similarities in situations and tasks, and recognizing common features helps us develop strategies and methods for coping with our world, in reality each situation and task is unique. We forget this, we go through life applying routine methods to routine problems and tasks, and life becomes stale. The beginner's way is to apply proven methods to the particulars of each task or situation. It is to recognize both the common and unique aspects of the situation and tailor the approach to the particular situation. In this way, our methods, techniques, and strategies for dealing with tasks and situations are ever changing and evolving. Each application of the method to the circumstances of the moment becomes a unique and compelling event. Each time a task is done with a proven technique it is a singular transaction between technique and task that unifies them in the moment.

Beginner's mind is an open, flexible, empty mind. This is especially important for learning. If the mind is filled with preconceptions, judgments, and irrelevancies, including thoughts of self, it is difficult to learn.

The Tyranny of the Ego

We all know people who have monster egos. These are people who think the sun shines only on them, others were placed on earth to admire them, life is a movie in which they are the star and everyone else is supporting cast, what they say and do matters to everyone, and their parents are very lucky to have them as children.

We all also know people who have ego monsters. These are people with fragile egos. They have low self-esteem. They think the sun shines on everyone but them, others were placed on earth so they can look bad by comparison, life is a movie that they can't get into, anything they say or do will only embarrass them, and their parents are humiliated to be related to them.

The monster ego is too full of himself to be fully involved with anything he is doing. If what life brings to be done in the moment does not enhance the ego by advertising his worth to the world, it is not worth doing. The task itself does not matter much to the monster ego. What matters is that it is he who is doing the task. The consequences of the task for his aggrandizement is the central concern.

Although students are adequately represented in the ranks of monster egos, these gargantuan egos are more often found in academia in the form of rigid professors who launch venomous attacks on anyone who questions their cherished position on an issue. These are people who have invested their entire leviathan egos in one or a few ideas, and they feel they will be ruined by a successful challenge. Of course, since they have so much ego riding on the idea, they see challenges everywhere. They assume a very defensive posture. For such men and women, a display of open-mindedness or tolerance for opposing views is not a chink in their armor, it is a gaping hole of vulnerability.

The man with an immense ego, let us call him Professor M. Ego, thinks his entire scholarly reputation is dependent on the strength of one or a few ideas, which, of course, he thinks are central to his field of study. Any idea of his must be defended at all costs. This may be especially difficult in the face of the most powerful adversary, valid contradictory evidence. There are a number of effective strategies available to Professor Ego. One of the most commonly used is to disregard or uncategorically dismiss any evidence that refutes his argument. If people do not agree with him, they are simply wrong.

It is being right that is so important to Professor Monster Ego. The threat of being wrong is so powerful that he closes his mind to any information that could potentially invalidate his claims. When his task at hand is researching and writing about a certain topic or issue, which is part of the mandate of most university professors, his mind is more on how his conclusions will affect his rightness rather than a search for and presentation of valid information. His concern with being right, and being viewed as right in the eyes of his colleagues and students, precludes him from doing his job of the moment right. Instead of being wholly involved in the moment and honestly and to the best of his ability assessing all the evidence that bears on the question of interest, Professor Monster Ego is massaging data, skirting issues, and bullying his juniors to insure that he is seen as right in the future. Professor M. Ego is precluded from discovering the joy of doing right what life brings to be done in the present because his mind is in the future. He is not mindful, that is, totally involved and aware, in the moment. Professor M. Ego may be right about a number of things. Despite his closed mind, his argument, claim, theory, or perspective may be right. And he may be held in high esteem by his peers and students because he is right. His effort, however, is not right.

Monster egos are usually more of a burden to others than to their possessors. Ego monsters, on the other hand, more often victimize their hosts than others. Nevertheless, those suffering from an ego monster can be exasperating to even the most tolerant souls.

Those with ego monsters are characterized by low self-esteem, fear of failure, repressed anger, and feelings of inadequacy. They avoid tests and challenges, stick to the well-trodden path, and abhor all that is novel. Instead of accepting what life brings to be done in the moment, they withdraw or operate within only a circumscribed life arena.

When attending school, the person who suffers from an ego monster, let us call him Mr. E. Monster, is convinced that he fails any test he takes. During his academic career, there are at least several tests that he never takes because he is immobilized by pretest anxiety and fear of failure. Student Monster drops at least a course a semester before he receives any evaluation from the professor on his performance because in his eyes his failure is a certainty. And he has to take all the difficult courses required for his degree in the last semester because he could not face them until he absolutely had to take them.

E. Monster's friends and roommates were sympathetic at the beginning of the semester. But now they find his incessant self-criticism, his constant lack of confidence, and his defeatist attitude grating. When E. Monster does well on an exam or paper, he cannot bring himself to take credit for it. He attributes his success to chance factors, mistakes, and the intervention of the gods. When he does consistently well, as many of those who are victims of ego monsters do, he is convinced that he will be found out to be a fraud and publicly humiliated.

E. Monster and M. Ego, at first glance, may appear to be very different kinds of people. They at least seem to be at different ends of a continuum. Actually, they are different sides of the same coin. Both suffer from the same malady: time-place dissonance caused by a preoccupation with self. The thoughts of the consequences of their actions for the self interfere with their contact with reality, and produce anxiety. In the case of M. Ego, anxiety is a call to action. E. Monster, on the other hand, is immobilized by it.

Several psychologists who have studied stress and anxiety point out that persons who inordinately engage in self-preoccupation and self-evaluation suffer from high anxiety. According to Norman Endler, a widely known expert on anxiety, "anxiety is related to self-evaluation . . . the highly anxious person is self-centered and focuses on self-evaluation and self-worry rather than on the situation task."

From the Zen perspective, it does not matter how your problem manifests itself or what you call it—Ego Monster, Monster Ego, Monster Shmonster. What matters is that you recognize the source of the problem is too much emphasis on you and not enough on what you are supposed to be doing. To solve the problem you have to start studying with right effort. You have to concentrate less on you and more on what you are doing. Even if you do not have a monster ego or an ego monster, the experience of studying with right effort will convince you it is the right way to study. Right effort is a way to educate the ego about its proper size and place.

Is There Life After Ego?

I have to admit that when I first encountered the notion of egolessness, I summarily and emphatically rejected the idea. It struck me as a loss of identity. It was the stuff of Orwell's *Nineteen Eighty-four*, and Huxley's *Brave New World*: everyone wearing the same suit, thinking the same thoughts, dreaming the same dreams. How boring!

The idea of egolessness spawned a number of threatening questions. Does taking thoughts of self or ego out of activities mean that people as unique individuals will vanish? Aren't thoughts of self needed to sustain sense of self and self-confidence? As I read and thought further, I realized that I had confused sense of self and self-confidence with being self-centered. I concluded that as you become less self-conscious and more conscious, you become more you than ever. And you express your "youness" or true self in everything you do. If you let the self or ego drop away, you are liberated from pretense and concerns with image and appearances. You become just you doing what needs to be done in the moment. Dropping thoughts of you from what you are doing is not a rejection of yourself. It is accepting yourself as you are in the moment.

We have all encountered people who just seem to be doing exactly what they should be doing at the time without a hint of self-consciousness, strain, or worry. Their effort appears effortless. They look as if they were put on earth to do what they are doing, and only the doing counts. Nothing else matters. Nothing else should matter. They seem sacred in the moment. They have always been there. They are wholly themselves and nothing else.

Marvelous moments occur when people are in a state of flow or peak performance. Whether the activity is tennis, painting, chess, gardening, or learning, it doesn't matter. When people are in a state of flow, they are wholly absorbed in what they are doing.

They are timeless in the moment. For them, there is only what they are doing in the moment. And no promise of gain or threat of pain could make them perform with more sincerity. Their doing is an expression of their deepest nature. They are what they are doing.

Carrots, Sticks, and Ego Trips

For some, especially those who subscribe or over-subscribe to the "looking out for Number 1" philosophy, an approach that deemphasizes ego is blasphemous. For others, those who cling to the eighteenth-century mechanistic model of human behavior, a perspective that does not prominently feature external rewards and punishments to motivate is ludicrous. Carrots and sticks, debits and credits, supply and demand, and the bottom line on the balance sheet are what make people tick.

While it is true that these are motivators for some people, particularly those who hold a worldview premised on rational-economic principles, it is not inconceivable that others do what needs to done in the moment for reasons other than self-interest in the sense of enhancing the ego or avoiding damage to it. No push or pull is needed.

Right effort or doing well what needs to be done in the moment, without anything extra, without thought of self or ego, does not mean that there are not reasons or purposes for doing what you are doing in the moment. If you are a student, you desire to obtain a college degree. Most students must study to pass examinations and to fulfill other degree requirements. Since you are a student, what life will bring you in the moment is books to be read, papers to be written, and tests to be taken. If you were a fireman, a fisherman, or a thespian, your moments would be occupied by different tasks.

Right effort means that your involvement in the task at hand is total. Carrots, sticks, and ego trips are irrelevant. It is too late to be thinking about them. The moment has arrived. What needs to be done needs doing. Life is presenting you with the kinds of tasks that you should be doing by virtue of your interest and goals. You need only do them as well as you can in the moment. Nothing else is needed. No carrots. No sticks. No ego trips. If you are a fireman, put out fires. If you are a fisherman, fish. If you are a thespian, act. If you are a student, dance with your books.

Doing well what needs to be done in the moment does not mean what you are doing is without instrumental merit. If the test for which you are preparing is important to obtaining your degree in accounting, for example, your studying has obvious practical benefits. And if you are studying something like accounting, you probably chose your program of study because of the tangible rewards associated with a degree in accounting.

Although preparing for a cost accounting exam, for instance, can have practical utility, if you are studying with right effort you are not thinking of it. The consequences of taking the exam for which you are studying should not be on your mind. The value of the accounting degree, the glee you will feel when you pass the exam, the humiliation, anger, and dejection you will feel if you fail the test, or any other thoughts of consequences interfere with your understanding of cost accounting in the moment. Cost accounting is the only thing that should matter. Thinking of anything else is extra. The preparation for the exam is the task at hand. It should command your complete attention.

As a way of avoiding time-place dissonance and promoting right effort, you should never consider one task a preparation for another. To consider something a preparation suggests that it does not have importance in its own right. Everything you do you should consider the most important thing in the world. It is because it is, at that moment, the only thing in the world.

Goal Displacement

Thinking about your reasons for doing something while you are doing it can not only be counterproductive but also can limit your chances of experiencing the joy of doing in the moment. Those who think about motives so often and intensely that they get strongly attached or stuck to them will never enjoy what they are doing for its intrinsic value. They will never enjoy an activity for itself.

An example will help clarify this point. Say you begin running to shed a few extra pounds. You read in a recent issue of *Super Self: The Magazine for Number 1* that the way to motivate yourself is to think that with each step you run you burn a portion of a calorie, which means that after you have run zillions of steps, those unsightly pounds, which are keeping you out of the fast lane, right crowd, and perfect relationship, will be gone. As you run, you chant the motivational mantra suggested in the article: "Kill those pounds. Burn them away. I'll look like a movie star in just five short days." The vision of a slim, successful, irresistible you is ever in your head as you pound along.

After great effort, you reach your target weight. Objective accomplished! Do you keep running? Not if your last run, like your first, was considered a painful means to a desirable end. But many people who start running to lose weight keep running even after the weight is lost. Why? Because in their effort to lose weight, they serendipitously discover running for the sake of running. This is what the well-known Harvard psychologist Gordon Allport called the "functional autonomy of motives." You start doing something for one reason, and you continue to do it for others.

Those who continue to run even after they have reached their desired weight (and presumably do not have to continue to run to maintain the weight loss) may find it difficult to articulate their reasons for continuing. They might have a vague notion that something to do with the act itself keeps them running.

And it keeps them running despite tender tendons, foul weather, and busy schedules. It defies rational explanation. It does not fit into any mechanistic carrot-stick model. There is something about the *doing* of running that beckons them to the streets, parks, and tracks. When they run, they become totally involved in their running. Some talk of their selves becoming immersed in the run. The run and the runner are one ... breath ... trees ... stride ... wind ... breath ... sky.

Of course, this does not happen to everyone. It is most unlikely to happen to those who tenaciously grip their goal of weight loss and the attendant benefit of physical attractiveness. The more you are attached to the future objective, the less likely you are to realize the benefits of what you are doing in the moment, which may not have a lot to do with your ultimate goal. Often in life, the journey is more important than the destination and process is more important than the product or outcome.

The product or outcome of the process in which you are currently involved is always in the future. Sometimes it is in the distant future. Usually many factors other than your effort affect it. Most of these factors are out of your control. The process is in the present. It is the doing in the moment. It is dealing with events as they unfold, moment by moment. This is where your attention should be. This is where you have some control. You can control how you approach the task. Of course, you do not have control over how events unfold, but you do have control over how you respond to events.

The Instability of Goals as a Foundation for Action

Many claim that strong goal orientation is the way to generate motivation. They suggest that thoughts of accomplishment and ego enhancement are needed as driving forces for completing necessary tasks. One problem with this approach is that commitment to goals and their attractiveness can vary, sometimes radically, over time. Even those who prize higher education and are committed to obtaining a college degree have days when they question their commitment and the value of education. As goal strength wanes, their motivation diminishes. This means that on days when goal strength is weak, and we all have those days, motivation will be correspondingly weak, and not much will be accomplished.

Right effort means a commitment to the work to be done in the moment rather than to the goal. It is not goal-dependent in the sense that if you work with right effort you do not rely on the daily, or even moment by moment, strength of your feelings about your goals to furnish you with the necessary motivation to do what needs doing. Your commitment is to doing well what needs to be done in the moment. Your duty is to do a quality job. Your emotional attachment to your goals may come and go; the job to be done in the moment remains. If you approach your task with the right attitude, it is your duty to do it well.

The Role of Goals

According to my friend and colleague Professor Todd Clear of Rutgers University, goals are not something to be accomplished; rather their purpose is to provide a general direction for your life. This means that goals can and should significantly influence your life moment to moment. Although your motivation and attitude toward the task of the moment should not be dependent on goals, what life brings to be done in the moment is not independent of goals. Your decision to go to school, for whatever reasons, shapes what you are faced with moment by moment. The task at hand would be very different if you were a butcher, a baker, or a microchip maker. Your goals are important. They should not go unexamined.

You should periodically review your goals, and evaluate how the decisions you have made and your performance relate to the realization of your goals. Are you taking the right courses with the right professors? Are you putting in the hours of study required to do well in each course? Is your social life or lack of one impinging on your school performance? All these questions reflect the larger issue of how seriously are you taking your education.

Sometimes you have to spring the big question. You have to ask yourself if school is the right place for you at this time in your life. Should you be doing something else rather than going to school? What should that something else be?

The problem with answering the big question is one of criteria. How do you know, for example, when you have given it enough time and effort? There are no universal criteria. You have to develop your own through honest self-examination.

My view, and I am admittedly biased, is that most students who decide that they have had enough of school have not put in sincere and genuine effort. In many cases, they are blocked from really trying by preconceptions about the value of education in general or the usefulness of a specific courses. "I mean, really, who cares what Ludwig Wittgenstein had to say in *Tractatus Logico-Philosophicus*? Isn't a tractatus logico-philosophicus a giant, log-eating, land lizard? Gross! I could never get into that. What can you do with knowledge about those things, anyway?"

Another major reason for not putting in the required effort to do well in school is fear of failure, an ego concern previously introduced. For any number of reasons, some students feel they are not smart enough or good enough to succeed in college, especially in some courses. While they may not always directly admit this to themselves, there is a lurking suspicion that they are not qualified to take a place in the classroom. If they do not put in a sincere effort, their ability or the extent of their disability always remains unknown. They might have done well if they had tried. If, on the other hand, they try and fail, they are without a doubt failures. And if they try and succeed, they must carry the burden of success. This is a high price for some, because it carries the expectation of success, and more important the sincere effort it requires, in the future. In any case, the consequences of their actions, instead of the actions themselves, are so much on the minds of these students that it is impossible for them to put in right effort.

I suspect that if most people do just about anything with right effort they will continue to do it. Consider all the compelling activities that are done in Japanese culture as an exercise in or expression of right effort: archery, flower arranging, brush painting, gardening, tea preparation and drinking, poetry writing, meditation, sword fighting, and unarmed combat. In other cultures dancing and chanting serve a similar purpose. In American culture, although activities have not been specifically designed to promote right effort and selflessness, the reports of some outdoor sportsmen, for example, fishermen, lead us to believe that proper pursuit is more important than the catch, despite all the stories about the big one that got away. Some people fish to fish. They will tell you that they lose themselves in fishing, and get back to some basic state where they feel connected with their surroundings. Fish, sky, pool, man, boat, pole, tree, water lily are all fishing.

Studying is an activity that if done with right effort can become as compelling as any of the activities commonly associated with the expression of right effort. When you study with right effort, as if you are fishing for knowledge or dancing with your books, studying gradually becomes less of a chore or grind and more of an expression of what should be the true relationship between you and school. You may not like studying all the time, but you will find it becomes such a compelling activity, like fishing or dancing, that your effort will be sustained. If this does not occur, it means either that your effort was not right effort or the activity, studying, is just not right for you.

If you have faithfully studied with right effort for at least one year, and you have never experienced the joy of understanding and learning, the ease of studying or writing when you are just cooking along on an assignment, or the grace and exhilaration of dancing with your books, it is time to reexamine your decision to enroll in school. First, however, you should examine your effort. Was your effort right? Did you study as if it were a sacred duty? Did you study with total involvement? Did you disregard feelings and other distractions when you studied?

Confusion, Uncertainty, and Disappointment

Do not be too quick to quit studying a subject or give up learning a new skill because you feel considerable confusion, doubt, or disappointment. It is not unusual to experience such feelings when doing just about anything in life that requires a sustained effort. These feelings can sometimes be the result of concentrating too much on goals or constantly comparing what is to what we thought would be. Goals and expectations are not what we are doing in the moment. They are not the reality of the here and now. They are at best abstractions of what will happen if everything goes according to plan. Since our plans and expectations are simplified versions of some desired future reality, the reality, when it arrives in all its complexity and richness, seldom matches our simple, usually one-dimensional, expectations. If you are too strongly attached to future expectations and you are constantly comparing some desirable state that you think should have arrived to what is, you often will be disappointed and confused by the gap between your expectation and reality.

The problem of expectation-reality dissonance is none other than a variation of time-place dissonance resulting from wrong effort. Too much effort is placed on what will be or what should be instead of what needs doing in the moment. We question the relevance of our actions to our goals to the point of counterproductivity. We become overwhelmed by confusion and doubt at the expense of getting the job done.

Another common problem that spawns doubt and confusion among students is having vague goals. Some people do not have clear reasons for studying a subject or learning a new skill. They may have a vague notion that it is the right thing to do, and they may observe that everyone they know is doing it. But they may not have any clearly articulated educational or career goals.

If you are such a person, do not worry too much about it. Learning is a better thing to be doing than many other things you can do when you are trying to figure out what to do with yourself. If what you are learning brings you to college, for example, you are exposed to a wide variety of ideas and people, and you are encouraged to question and explore. Just take what comes in the moment, and do your best.

Keep in mind that your reasons for doing things, along with everything else in life, can change over time. You might go along taking a wide variety of courses for a while, and then one day it will dawn on you that you would like to write, for example, for a living. From this point on, writing will shape what is brought to you to be done in the moment, but it should not change your effort. Your effort should be right whether you have a definite goal in mind or some vague notion of how you want to spend some part of your life.

Even as your right effort and understanding of self ripen, you will still sometimes experience doubt and confusion. You might question the sincerity of your effort or the wisdom of trying to do things with right effort at all. Was not your old way of effort good enough? Is right effort worth the effort? Such questions are common in Zen training. Some Zen masters stress that great doubt is pivotal in attaining enlightenment. It produces the tension needed to break through to the point where great doubt is accepted, as is everything else in the world.

While great doubt is not necessary for understanding a subject or learning a new skill, doubt and confusion are common enough that you should learn to accept them and use them to your advantage. When doubt comes and you feel unsettled or nervous, and you have trouble letting these feelings go, try converting these feelings into tautness and awareness to be applied to whatever you are studying in the moment. Simply redefine them.

Rest assured that doubt and ambiguity are part of the complexity of life. To some extent, they will arise in everything you do. Once you accept them as such, they lose much of their power.

Zen and the Liberal Arts

Although any topic or program of study can be pursued with right effort, there is a traditional course of study in our universities that features many of the elements of the Zen approach as described in this book. Liberal arts education, in its true sense, promotes right effort. In the liberal arts tradition, studying is the expression of excellence and the development of virtue and understanding of self. The act of studying or writing in the moment is of primary importance. The acquisition of knowledge for utilitarian purposes is not stressed. However, there are not too many fields of study in which there are not some extrinsic benefits attached to the pursuit of intrinsic rewards.

There is nothing wrong with going to school for utilitarian reasons, such as career advancement. Your reason for going to school does not preclude the application of right effort to your studies. The pivotal element in determining whether your education is liberal is your attitude or approach. According to Donald L.

Levine, a dean at the University of Chicago, the idea of liberality in education is reflected in "the sense of a lifelong quest for perfection, wherein each moment is intrinsically satisfying, but the experience is framed as part of an unlimited pursuit of growth and improved expression." This is right effort. It is doing as perfectly as possible what life brings to be done in the moment as an expression of our human spirit. It is doing well what needs to be done for its own sake.

Most people do not learn something for liberal or nonutilitarian reasons, and most college students do not select liberal arts as their major. Declaring biology or business administration as your major or taking a practical course in automotive repair should not stop you from taking a liberal arts approach to learning. Whatever you study, you should study as if your studying in the moment is an expression of your deepest nature, like the artist painting or the dancer dancing.

One of the most clearly utilitarian groups of students is adult students returning to school. Their reason for attending school is some variation on either obtaining credentials for job advancement or acquiring requisite skills and degrees for changing careers. These students usually work full-time while attending school, and often have family responsibilities. If education did not have definite, almost guaranteed instrumental value, they would not be enrolled in school. If they did not constantly remind themselves of the instrumental value, they could not drag themselves to class after a full day on the job. Am I going to tell these students that they should become less utilitarian? Do I dare tell them to place less emphasis on outcome and more on process? Am I nuts to tell them to become more liberal and less goal-directed in their pursuit of education? What the heck!

If you are a returning adult student who (1) works eight or more hours a day at a job you hate, (2) has to get up to feed the baby four times a night, (3) never gets more the four hours of sleep, (4) has mortgage payments, car payments, insurance payments, tuition payments, and payments on the loan you took out to pay all the other payments, and (5) is going to school to get a better job that pays more money, I recommend that you forget about your reasons for going to school, and just study with right effort. I also recommend that you do not punch me in the head if you ever meet me.

I know it sounds crazy to suggest that you put aside your very reason for being in school. But once you start studying with right effort, I do not believe that you will need to keep the reason in mind at all times to motivate you to continue. And until you get the reason out of your mind, you will not be able to study with right effort or take a liberal approach to education.

If you are a returning adult student, you are usually making great sacrifices to continue your education. It isn't easy. You are often frustrated and always tired. Acquiring the right attitude and studying with right effort is especially important for you. You are putting so much into it. Why wait to get something out of it? Study with right effort. Benefit as you study.

The tangible benefits to be accrued from your academic efforts, for example, a rewarding career, will not materialize until you graduate. This means it can be years before you reap what you sow from your education. But you don't have to wait this long to get something from your education. If you concentrate on the sowing, you reap as you sow. In other words, if you want to be sure to get something now from your effort, concentrate on the effort itself, not on its consequences. Make the process of acquiring knowledge about any subject a work of art. Make your effort right. Your books summon you to dance. Now!

Discovering What Works

Buddha, Gautama Siddhartha, said on his deathbed, "Work out your own salvation with diligence." His words have been interpreted to mean that realization or enlightenment will be attained neither by uncritically accepting authoritative interpretations of the scriptures nor by blindly following the prescriptions of others. True knowledge can only be acquired through the application of universal, time-tested principles to one's own life. In other words, to make them living principles, rather than stale and worn platitudes, you must actually discover for yourself, in your own way, what the enlightened ones before you have discovered. The knowledge abides in you waiting to be discovered. Look to yourself, not outside, to breathe life into what resides within.

My view is that within each of us is a real student. People are by nature seekers of knowledge, explorers. Our natural talent or propensity is sometimes hidden or constrained by any number of attachments to ego or by illusions we have developed about ourselves over the years. In order to pursue knowledge, we must free ourselves from these attachments and illusions, and learn to study with right effort. This usually requires some program to be followed systematically to develop the right attitudes and skills.

The bulk of the remaining sections of this book will consist of discussions of problems commonly encountered in trying to study with right effort and descriptions of exercises and techniques that foster right effort or mindfulness. They are intended to create conditions that promote total absorption in studying, or "flow states." It is your responsibility to cull from the material presented and other materials you have available a program that is right for you. No one can do this for you. You must bring the suggestions presented to life by fashioning them into a routine and following that routine without fail.

In following your program, you will constantly make new discoveries. Your program is not something to be followed ritualistically. It must be allowed to grow and change to survive. Your program must have life to sustain your interest. You need room to maneuver. But you also need structure and commitment. You have to stick with your program through good times and bad to allow it to reach maturity. You cannot stop because it becomes difficult, boring, or frustrating. As was pointed out in the beginning of this book, the two important rules in following the path are "Begin" and "Walk on." The path is the same for everyone, but each person's footsteps are different. The most important point to remember is that no one can walk the path for you. Others can merely point to the way.

Part Two

CLEARING AND CALMING THE MIND

Meditation: Purpose and Results

One practice that should be incorporated into everyone's program of study is daily meditation. As a preparatory exercise for studying, meditation will serve as a method to clear your mind. The purpose of meditating is to relax and silence the constant internal dialogue that goes on in your mind so you can devote your full attention to studying. It is a way to recognize the din of idle chatter and noise in your mind and begin to quiet it. When you first start meditating, sometimes you will be astonished at the number and speed of thoughts that race through your mind as you try to sit quietly. Sometimes they will be like jet-propelled popcorn exploding into consciousness and zooming around. At other times, they will be more like marshmallow clouds drifting into conciousness and sticking in your mind. Or thoughts may come in waves, either gently rolling in and eroding concentration or violently crashing in and disturbing tranquility.

The practice of meditation is to disregard all thoughts. Don't pay attention to any of them. Just let them go. Don't attach or cling to them. The result is a mind like still water or a clear blue sky.

After your meditation ripens and matures, you will discover that it serves purposes other than just clearing your mind and helping you to relax before studying. In his informative book on meditation, Lawrence LeShan, a practicing therapist who has explored the therapeutic value of meditation, discusses two major results of meditation: greater efficiency and enthusiasm in daily life, and the acquisition of a new view or comprehension of reality.

LeShan presents the first result, more competent task performance, as a consequence of meditation enhancing our ability to accomplish tasks with right effort. According to LeShan,

> Much of the work of any form of meditation is in learning to do one thing at a time: if you are thinking about something to be just thinking of it and nothing else; if you are dancing to be just dancing and not thinking about your dancing. This kind of exercise certainly produces more efficiency at anything we do rather than less.
>
> Tuning and training the mind as the athlete tunes and trains the body is one of the primary aims of all forms of meditation. This is one of the basic reasons that this discipline increases efficiency in everyday life.

LeShan also points out that meditation increases our efficiency and enthusiasm in everyday life because it helps us deal with anxiety and other impediments to performance. In this way meditation has practical benefits because of its therapeutic effects.

The second product of meditation, a different view of reality, is more difficult to validate externally than the more practical consequence of greater efficiency in everyday life. This different perspective is commonly referred to as a higher state of consciousness, or expanded consciousness, and it has been prized by mystics of all persuasions for centuries—Zen, Christian, Hebrew, and Indian, to name a few. A number of names are associated with this higher view of reality, and there are a number of ways to achieve it. Generally, however, all forms or versions of this different view include the abolition of the ego or separate self, as we commonly know it, and the realization of the oneness of the universe. It is a return to a primordial state of wholeness.

It is not readily apparent that the comprehension of

a different view of reality, spiritually going home or discovering oneness with the universe, can have practical benefits. Mysticism is seldom listed among the down-to-earth, nuts-and-bolts, no-nonsense approaches to taking care of business. But psychological benefits accrue from both the mystical and practical results of meditation. An example of an effect of meditation that has both practical and mystical relevance is unification of the mind. Unification is a mental state that is necessary for the acquisition of a new perspective or enlightenment. The unification of the mind achieved through meditation concentrates and integrates the energy of the mind. There are obvious practical benefits when the unified mind is applied to the tasks of every day life, including studying.

Most readers will agree that the benefits of meditation are attractive. Meditation, however, can be a long, difficult road that must be traveled every day no matter what the conditions. The next section will tell you how to begin. Walking on is completely up to you.

Meditation: Practice

The ultimate purpose of meditation is to quiet the mind so in the resulting silence we can realize that which already exists within each of us. Out of the darkness and quiet comes the light of understanding. Our immediate practical purpose in meditating is to calm, clear, and unify the mind as a preparation for studying. Meditation for this reason is not unusual before many activities in some cultures. For example, some martial artists meditate before combat or practice, and Japanese artists try to achieve a state of perfect calm that will be reflected in their art.

Although meditation is a purposeful activity for you in that you want to achieve a state of mental clarity and relaxation, you should not be concerned with the purposes of meditation or anything else when you are meditating. Meditation practice is the practice of right effort. When you meditate, just meditate. Do not think of why you are meditating or how well you are meditating. Just meditate. Do not think of what you will gain from meditation. Just meditate.

A simple form of Zen sitting meditation (zazen) is the practice of breath counting. This practice is easy to describe and the mechanics of the technique are easily grasped, but as you will see, it is difficult to do. Do not be misled by its simplicity. It has been practiced for thousands of years, and some Zen students practice this simple form of meditation for a lifetime.

The daily practice of meditation teaches you to do one thing at a time. When you meditate properly you give your undivided attention to one activity. Meditation can be seen as the practice of concentration in a very limited activity. What could be more limited than sitting and breathing? The idea is just to sit and breathe as we are, without concern for anything else. Gradually, the powers of concentration, or one-pointedness, cultivated in meditation generalize to other activities, in our case, learning.

The practice of zazen for the purpose of developing concentration is called *bompu* Zen by Master Yasutani. *Bompu* means ordinary. It is the practice of meditation for strictly practical reasons, that is, there are no philosophical or religious underpinnings. It appears to be uniquely suited for Western students.

Bompu Zen, being free from any philosophic or religious content, is for anybody and everybody. It is a Zen practiced purely in the belief that it can improve both physical and mental health . . .

Through the practice of bompu Zen you learn to concentrate and control your mind. It never occurs to most people to try to control their minds, and unfortunately this basic training is left out of contemporary education, not being part of what is called the acquisition of knowledge. Yet without it what we learn is difficult to retain because we learn it improperly, wasting much energy in the process. Indeed, we are virtually crippled unless we know how to restrain our thoughts and concentrate our minds. Furthermore, by practicing this very excellent mode of mind training you will find yourself increasingly able to resist temptations to which you had previously succumbed, and to sever attachments which had long held you in bondage. An enrichment of personality and a strengthening of character inevitably follow since the three basic elements—that is, intellect, feeling, and will— develop harmoniously.

The next few pages will contain a description of the practice of breath counting as a form of zazen. The presentation will be organized into the three related elements, or what Master Taisen Deshimaru calls the essence of zazen: posture, breathing, and attitude of mind.

Posture

Flopping down in your favorite overstuffed chair and hanging your leg over its arm may be relaxing, but it is not proper posture for zazen. Indeed, the position is really not that comfortable. Don't take my word for it. Flop into your favorite chair, and try to sit still for five minutes. Comfy? Relaxed? I doubt it. I suspect in a couple of minutes, you'll find that you want to switch some part of your body to a new position. The zazen positions that are described below are designed for the long haul. In these positions, you can sit still for long periods of time without putting pressure on internal organs or producing tension in your muscles. I'm not claiming that there is no discomfort associated with zazen positions, especially during the initial stages of your meditation program. I am saying for sitting very still, alert, and relaxed, you can't beat these zazen positions.

The zazen positions that will be described in this section reflect and help produce the proper state of mind for practicing zazen. These positions are intended to create harmonious unification of body and mind and promote concentration, or one-pointedness.

They foster the attitude of relaxed alertness that is the hallmark of zazen. They are positions that are well suited for practicing moment-to-moment awareness.

Once you have learned to sit and you have been practicing for a while, you can perform an experiment that should convince you of the importance of proper posture. Sit in the proper way for a few minutes, and then sit improperly for a few minutes. Notice the difference in your breathing and concentration.

Several positions can be taken for zazen. The best one for you depends on your physical condition, most importantly your flexibility. There even may be times when you use more than one sitting position in a single meditation period.

The five sitting positions are full-lotus; half-lotus; Burmese, or tailor; seiza, or traditional Japanese kneeling posture; and sitting in a chair. The first four of these positions are illustrated on the next page.

Full-lotus, the most demanding position, requires that you place your right foot with sole up over your left thigh and vice versa for the left. With you legs in this pretzel shape, both of your knees should be touching the ground. The full-lotus provides a wide base for sitting, and it is the most stable of all positions. When you are trying to concentrate fully on the activity of the moment, in this case, just sitting, stability is important. Any wobbling or wavering will interfere with your ability to calm and unify your mind.

While it is the most desirable sitting position, the full-lotus position is not for everyone. It certainly is not for me. The half-lotus is a reasonable alternative for some meditators who have difficulty with the full-lotus. To get into the half-lotus, place the right foot over the left thigh, just as described for the full lotus. Then place the left foot under the right thigh. You can switch the position of the left and right legs during meditation if you need to.

The half-lotus is another position that is not for me and a lot of other people. The Burmese, or tailor, position requires less flexibility, and it is a lot easier on the knees than are the full- and half-lotus posi-

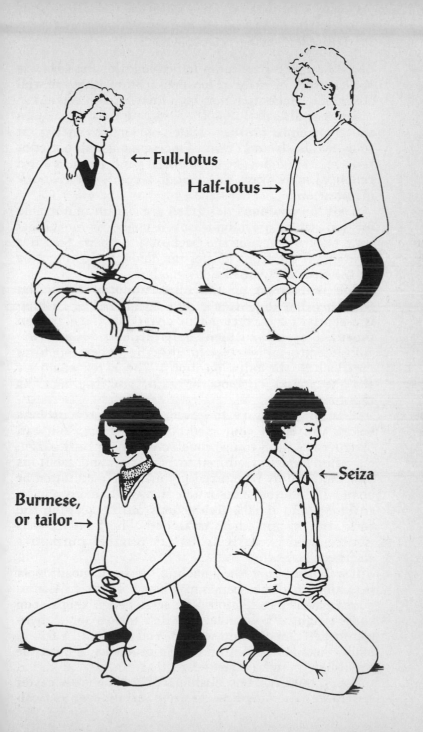

← Full-lotus

Half-lotus →

Burmese, or tailor →

← Seiza

tions. In the Burmese or tailor posture, the legs are not crossed. Simply place one foot in front of the other, and make sure that both knees touch the mat.

Another alternative is the seiza, or traditional Japanese kneeling posture, which is simply sitting on your own heels and calves. Placing a cushion between your legs so you are straddling it, and using a seiza bench, also are ways to maintain a comfortable kneeling position.

If all the positions described are too uncomfortable for you, sit in a straight-backed chair. Do not allow your back to rest on the back of the chair. Sit on a cushion on the front half of the chair. Keep your feet on the floor and your back straight.

You will notice in the illustrations of the zazen positions that the sitter is on a cushion. The cushion is essential for correct posture. Without the elevation provided by the cushion, it is difficult to keep the spine comfortably straight and the knees touching the floor in the lotus positions. The zazen cushions are the round cushion, or zafu, and the mat, or zabuton.

It is not necessary to buy or make these cushions before you begin your meditation program. You can improvise. I used to use couch cushions for my zazen, but after I was introduced to real zafus and zabutons at a Zen center, I acquired my own for meditation at home. I find the zafu much firmer than my couch cushions, and it is a tremendous aid in keeping the back straight and knees grounded. The family couch is now used exclusively for its original purpose—afternoon naps.

If you find that the kneeling, or seiza, position is best for you, a seiza bench may be a valued addition to your furniture collection. The seiza bench keeps your body weight off your legs, which makes for a more comfortable meditation session. You can build a homemade seiza bench with a couple of stacks of books of equal height and a short board.

You should not buy cushions or a bench when you first begin your meditation program. Indeed, you can do just fine without purchasing any aids. But if you intend to buy aids, make sure zazen is for you before making the investment.

Most of the Zen masters who have written about posture emphasize the importance of keeping your back straight while sitting. Robert Aitken, a contemporary American Zen master, suggests a one-year-old as a model for correct meditation posture. The baby sits up straight with his belly sticking out in front and his butt sticking out at the other end. This gives a slight curvature to the spine at the waist and keeps the upper body straight but relaxed. Your head should be straight, as if you are holding up the sky with the back of the top of your head. This will keep your chin in, your ears in line with your relaxed shoulders, and your nose and navel in line.

Your eyes should be lowered but open and unfocused. Gaze about three feet in front of you, but do not look at anything in particular. Your mouth should be closed, and your tongue should rest gently on the back of your upper teeth.

The position of the hands is also important in zazen. They should form what is called a mudra. It is formed by placing, with palms up, the left hand inside the right with the middle joint of the left middle finger directly on top of the middle joint of the right middle finger and the thumbs lightly touching. Sometimes it helps to think that you are holding an egg or a small cylinder in your hands.

When you sit, your hands should rest gently in your lap with your thumbs about the height of your navel. Your elbows should be held in a relaxed position a bit away from your body.

Once you have the knowledge and simple gear required to do zazen, the next question that arises is where to do it. The broadest answer is do it wherever you can. If the only time you can do zazen is in the library before your second class of the day, do it inconspicuously in the library. Find a chair in a remote place and meditate. Do not draw attention to yourself by meditating in full-lotus position in the middle of the library lounge. This is not meditating. It is performing.

If you have enough flexibility in your schedule and access to a number of private places, you should meditate in the quietest place. Select a place where there are very few distractions and you know you will not be interrupted. Wear comfortable, loose-fitting clothing when doing zazen, and always remove your shoes.

Breathing

In order for your breathing to be right, your zazen posture must be right. The instructions for breathing are simple. Just breathe naturally with the diaphragm and through the nose. Your exhale should be longer than your inhale, and your breathing should be smooth and effortless. Don't try to force smooth, deep breathing, however. Just go with the flow. If you are having a day when your breaths are short, don't be concerned. Just sit and breathe.

Most of us are unaccustomed to breathing with our diaphragm, and it may feel awkward at first. One visualization technique to promote correct breathing that some Zen masters recommend for beginners is to imagine that your breath is entering and exiting your body about two inches below your navel. This will not only help you to breathe with your diaphragm but also help keep your attention centered on your breath.

Now that you know how to sit and breathe properly, you can start to meditate. The simplest method is breath counting. Simply count your exhalations up to ten, and then begin over again. If you lose count, start over again at one. Do not try to estimate where you are in the sequence. You should start by doing this exercise for five minutes, and increase your zazen sessions by about one minute a week, until you reach twenty minutes. If you like, you can continue to increase your sessions to forty minutes or sit for more than one session a day.

When you first begin to practice zazen, you may often find yourself wondering how much time has passed as you sit. Thoughts about time can be especially intrusive if you do your timekeeping with a conventional watch, which you have to look at to see the time. You are much better off if you use some kind of alarm, for example, an alarm clock, a wristwatch alarm, or a kitchen timer, to keep time. This way it is easier to forget about the time. You can let time go, and let the mechanical or electronic device take care of it.

Of course, your timing device itself can be a distraction; a clock may tick loudly or the alarm may startle you. You can usually modify loudness by placing a towel over your timer. You still will be able to hear the alarm, but the ticking will not be distracting, and you will not be jolted out of meditation when your time is up.

I use my Casio electronic watch to time my meditation. This watch, which only cost about twenty dollars, has a countdown alarm operation that is almost perfect for timing meditation. I set it for the time I desire to meditate, and when that time is up, a gentle beeping sounds. Its only drawback is it marks every ten minutes that passes with one short beep. But this is not too distracting.

Schedule your daily meditation for any time you can conveniently fit it in. I think the morning, soon after rising, is best. Your mind is at its clearest. It is not yet cluttered with the events and pressures of the day. And starting the day with the unity, clarity, and serenity that results from meditation is a good way to begin especially hectic days. The one time you should not meditate is just after eating. Give yourself an hour or so to digest your food.

Attitude of Mind

Sitting zazen is your first practice in right effort. You must be aware of what you are doing, and totally invest in it without thought of consequences. To sit and lull yourself into a trance with absentminded mechanical counting of breaths is not zazen. Proper zazen requires that you be alert yet relaxed. The aim of zazen is not an inactive mind, but a calm, unified, open mind. As you count your breaths, you become them. You do not think one, two, three . . . , you become one, fully and completely. Then you are two. You sink into it. There is only two. Then you are three. There is nothing else. It permeates your body and mind. It fills the universe.

Thoughts will naturally arise when you are doing zazen, especially when you first start practicing. Do not try to suppress thoughts. Just let them go. Do not become attached to them, and they will disappear. Random thoughts are inevitable when you practice zazen. You should not be concerned with them. You are not unconscious when you meditate, and you should expect thoughts to occur. Thoughts only become a problem when you cling to them or chase after them and get into a thought process or a train of thought. Once you think about a thought by evaluating it as good or bad or linking it with another thought, you are in trouble.

One strategy for dealing with thoughts is to remind yourself before you begin your zazen that when you find yourself engaged in thought, you will stop counting, return to one, and start over again. It is important not to fall into the self-criticism trap each time you start over. Self-criticism can get you into a train of thought that takes you away from the main business of zazen—just sitting.

You should stop counting and return to one each time you pursue an inevitable random thought and you get involved in a sequence of thoughts or train of thought. A sequence of thoughts occurs when a single thought, say a paper you have to write, comes into consciousness when you are meditating and instead of letting it go you allow it to spawn another thought, like how far behind you are on the paper. Before you know it, you are in a full-blown thought episode about some future event, for example, never completing the paper, that takes you far away from what you are supposed to be doing in the moment, that is, just sitting and counting your breaths.

Most Zen masters who have written about meditation techniques suggest that when a thought arises during zazen, you should simply observe that a thought has arrived, and let it go. They point out that in zazen the idea is not to hold back or block out thoughts. Zazen is not an exercise in not thinking in the sense that you consciously and forcefully do not think. Not to think is impossible because to attempt it requires that you think about not thinking, and the intentional effort to suppress thought is, of course, thinking.

An accurate characterization of the state of mind proper for zazen is without-thinking. In without-thinking, you just accept what comes to mind without attaching to it, that is, without reflecting on it, objectifying it, or classifying it. You merely accept its presence and let it pass on naturally as all things do. Don't stop it and try to analyze it. Let it take its natural course, like the exhaled breath dissolving back into the undifferentiated atmosphere from which it came.

The whole point of zazen is to do only zazen when doing zazen, which means that you sit for a specified period of time without thinking. It is not a time to plan your day, work out a problem, or have a juicy fantasy. The task to be done in the moment when doing zazen is to sit in the correct posture and count breaths. This is all you should be doing. Anything else is extra, and it takes away from your zazen. If zazen is practiced properly and regularly, gradually the waves of the mind will be stilled, and you will reach a state in which your mind becomes like clear, calm water.

Meditation: Pitfalls and Problems

In this section, a number of the more common difficulties that may disturb your meditation will be discussed. Many of these difficulties are common impediments to doing any task with right effort, and in later sections they will be discussed specifically in relation to studying.

Two related pitfalls are high expectations and concern with progress. These problems arise when there is great emphasis on ends at the expense of means. When you take account of some of the results of zazen that have been described, it is easy to see how students can become attached to some ideal that they would like to achieve. Consider, for example, Peter Matthiessen's description of one of his satori (awakening) experiences:

> ... on this morning, in the near darkness—the altar candle was the only light in the long room—this immense hush swelled and swelled and kept on swelling, as if this "I" were opening out into infinity, in eternal amplification of my buddha being. There was no hallucination, only awe, "I" had vanished and also "I" was everywhere.
>
> Then I let my breath go, gave my self up to immersion in all things, to a joyous *belonging* so overwhelming that tears of relief poured from my eyes. For the first time since unremembered childhood, I was not alone, there was no separate "I." Wounds, anger, ragged edges, hollow places were all gone, all had been healed; my heart was the heart of all creation. *Nothing was needed*, nothing missing, all was already, always, and forever present and forever known.

Who wouldn't count a few zillion breaths and sit until their legs atrophied for such an enlightenment experience? Most of us would be willing to settle for the less marvelous results described by Master Yasutani:

> With body and mind consolidated, focused, and energized, the emotions respond with increased sensitivity and purity, and volition exerts itself with greater strength of purpose. No longer are we dominated by intellect at the expense of feeling, nor driven by the emotions unchecked by reason or will. Eventually za-

zen leads to a transformation of personality and character. Dryness, rigidity, and self-centeredness give way to flowing warmth, resiliency, and compassion, while self-indulgence and fear are transmuted into self-mastery and courage.

While these results of zazen are considered pearls of great value by most, as is even our more modest goal of a clear and calm mind for studying, if you keep your eyes on the pearls instead of your breath and posture, the pearls will never be yours. The obvious reason for this is that focusing on results, which are always in the future, takes your attention away from the process of meditation in the present. In order to realize the results of meditation, your full attention must be devoted to the act of meditating in the present.

The related pitfall of always gauging your progress also takes you away from the task of the moment—sitting and breathing with total involvement. If you constantly worry about how you are doing, your whole effort will not be put into doing it. Usually when you evaluate your progress, you conclude that you are not progressing fast enough. This kind of assessment plants the seeds for disturbing thoughts during meditation. The correct view of progress is to assume it will be gradual. Looking for dramatic results in meditation will result only in disappointment. Although during some periods, often when you first start meditating, progress will seem rapid and meditation sessions may seem marvelous, these sensations will not last. You should not expect your meditation to be consistently good or to improve with each sitting. Although enlightenment or realizations occurs in flashes, meditation should be approached as a journey taken step by methodical, all-encompassing step.

One precaution that should be taken to avoid emphasis on progress and dramatic results is to limit the amount of talking you do about your meditation, except with your teacher, of course, if you have one. When you discuss your meditation with other meditators, you risk making invidious and insidious comparisons. The result is that you conclude that your meditation is either superior or inferior to that of others. These implicit judgments made during conversation will emerge as disturbing thoughts during your meditation.

Once you start discussing your meditation with others on a regular basis, you may begin to generate a set of implicit benchmarks. When this happens, you are in danger of falling into the trap of the "have-you-experienced-this-one-yet game." Your meditation is no longer a personal journey in which each step counts. It becomes a race in which you dash to experience some sensation that has very little to do with the real work of meditation.

If you meditate with a group, some discussion will be natural. In some situations, refusing to discuss your meditation is cold and selfish. Indeed, discussions among groups of meditators who are earnest and sincere can be beneficial. In such situations, you should contribute to the discussion, but always be aware of the potential dangers of making comparisons and measuring progress.

High expectation and a focus on progress can lead to what Robert Aitken calls the "spiritual desert." It is a place where you stand alone and come face to face with your doubt: "Why meditate? Where is it getting me? If I had used the time I spent sitting counting my breaths playing the stock market, I might be rich. Is this meditation stuff some cruel joke conjured up by a bunch of swamis drinking at a swami convention?"

If the student is a seasoned meditator and the doubt is great, the "spiritual desert" may be the darkness before the dawn or the "sick soul" experienced by some people just before they reach realization. However, in the case of a beginner, it represents just another onslaught of disturbing thoughts that must be recognized for what they are and allowed to go on their way, dissipating into the air, so meditation can continue. Students have reported a variety of sensations while meditating. Some are quite pleasant, like floating, warmth, and visions of colors. Others are irritating and sometimes disturbing. Collectively they are known as *mayko*, and although they can be very compelling, they should be treated like any other thought that arises. Recognize them for what they are, and continue with your practice. As long as you do not attach or cling to them, they will not interfere with your practice.

Any *mayko* you encounter early in your practice will be relatively mild, and some people never experience mayko even at very advanced stages. So don't worry. You are not going to hallucinate a monster with the head of your third-grade teacher and the body of a pit bull terrier. You are, however, very likely to become engrossed in some fantasy that comes to mind while you are counting breaths.

Fantasies are both subtle and seductive. You can become fully involved in a fantasy while doing zazen without knowing exactly when you strayed from breath counting. It seems sometimes they emerge full-blown and invite you to take the part that is so right for you. When you find yourself in the clutches of a good fantasy, just stop following it, and get back to breath counting. Zazen is for sitting and breath counting. Just that. Nothing else. Fantasize on somebody else's time.

Personal problems are another source of disturbance while you are sitting. When thoughts of personal problems emerge during zazen, they can be especially disruptive because they are invested with so much emotion. Strong feelings of anger, resentment, frustration, anxiety, and hopelessness may be triggered by dwelling on personal problems during meditation.

At times, you may even have valid and beneficial insights into problems while meditating. All thoughts you have while meditating should be treated alike. It does not matter if they are positive or negative, pleasant or painful, useful or frivolous. You should not invest them with the power to disturb your meditation by attaching any significance to them. Just note that they have entered your consciousness, and get back to concentrating on your breath.

Even when thoughts or their associated emotions persist, continue with your zazen. Everyone has days when they are especially irritable and they feel as if they have hornets in their brain or red ants in their nervous system. When you have such a day, or even if you are chronically irritated, continue with your practice. Do not become preoccupied with your personal condition, no matter what it may be.

A problem I often encounter in my meditation is that I get anxious to get done with my meditation and get on with the business of the day. I'm like the runner who rushes through or skips his warm-ups so he can get on with his run, then longs for the end of the run all through it, so he can get on with his day. This approach to running, meditation, or studying puts one deeply in the pit of time-place dissonance. If you are always thinking a step ahead of where you are, you are out of sync, your mind and body are not unified, and you are not centered in the moment.

Thinking of your meditation or anything else you do as a preparation for something else is a common mistake. It brings the something else to the forefront of your mind, and takes your attention away from what you are doing. If you think of your meditation as a preparation for doing the business of the day, thoughts of the business of the day will disturb your meditation. You will find that you become impatient with your meditation. The business of the day awaits you. The real world beckons. Your meditation becomes an irritating chore. You start meditating perfunctorily. Then, not at all.

The way to limit intrusive thoughts about the business of the day and remain mindful, alert, and in the moment during your meditation is to look upon your meditation as part of the business of the day that is just as important as any other business you plan to do. Do not consider anything, including your meditation, a preparation for anything else. Everything you do should be considered an end in itself.

You should not feel that your meditation is taking time away from the important activities and tasks on your daily schedule. Your meditation is as deserving of your attention as any other daily task. Approach your meditation as earnestly as anything else you do.

You will inevitably experience some physical discomfort and pain during your meditation, especially when you are a beginner. As your meditation matures, so will your flexibility, and the amount of discomfort you feel in your legs while meditating will diminish. Don't be afraid of a little pain. Treat it like any other sensation you have while meditating. Accept its presence and get on with your breath counting. Don't get stuck thinking about your discomfort.

Sometimes pain is a sign that your posture is not right, especially if the pain is in the back or neck. In these cases, adjust your posture and see if the pain subsides. Sometimes you may want to switch positions, for example, from full-lotus to half-lotus, to reduce pain.

It important to keep in mind that zazen is not training for masochists or a test of one's ability to endure pain. You should not get stuck on the idea of finishing your meditation session in the position you started at all costs. Adjust your position or switch positions when necessary. But don't be too quick to make changes. Try accepting mild pain or discomfort and going on with your meditation.

Meditation: A Recapitulation

The three preceding sections have contained a great deal of information about meditation, and it may appear to be a formidable task to remember and apply it all to your daily meditation. The purpose of this summary is to make the task more manageable by trimming the mass of information to a few handfuls of essential points. They are presented in a form that is intended for quick review before sitting.

I. Posture
   1. Back straight
   2. Chin in
   3. Ears in line with shoulders
   4. Back of head holding up the sky
   5. Eyes open, cast downward, unfocused
   6. Hands in mudra, left palm inside right, thumbs lightly touching
   7. Knees providing a firm base by touching the ground

II. Breathing
   1. Natural
   2. Inhale and exhale through nose
   3. Use diaphragm
   4. Imagine breath coming in and out just below navel
   5. Count each exhalation to ten and start again
   6. Do not count mechanically or absentmindedly
   7. Each breath is a singular, all-encompassing event
   8. Become each breath

III. Attitude or Mind-set
   1. Alert, taut, attentive, absorbed
   2. Sink into your breathing
   3. There is only breathing; just sitting breathing is the task at hand
   4. Do not suppress thoughts and images, but do not cling to them; just let them go and return to breath counting
   5. Don't worry about achieving anything in zazen, just sit, don't measure your progress, just count your breaths

If you faithfully follow these instructions and meditate every day with sincerity and humility, you will notice that gradually you experience more clarity of mind, patience, serenity, and acuity.

Breath counting is not the only form of zazen. Koan meditation, in which the meditator focuses on a Zen problem or riddle, and skikan-taza, which is "just sitting" without concentrating on anything special, are other forms of zazen. These, however, should be practiced with the guidance of a qualified teacher.

Obviously, there are many forms of meditation other than zazen. Indeed, the great number and variety of forms of meditation attest to its importance and universality. Some additional meditation practices that can help you relax or deal with specific problems you might have with your studies are suggested later in this book. If you are interested in exploring a variety of meditation techniques, read *The Fine Arts of Relaxation, Concentration and Meditation: Ancient Skills for Modern Minds* by Joel Levey, and *How to Meditate: A Guide to Self-Discovery* by Lawrence LeShan.

Zen in the Shower

One view of zazen, as previously mentioned, is the application of right effort to a very restricted activity, that is, sitting and breathing. It is the practice of becoming wholly absorbed in the moment and the task at hand. You, the moment, and the task become one. There is a recognized or realized unity of person, time, and activity.

Obviously, right effort should not be restricted to the meditation cushion. The purpose of this book is to help you study with right effort. And the whole point of Zen is the application of right effort to everything we do. As Peter Matthiessen puts it, "the application of zazen to the 'ordinary' world is the real point of this extraordinary practice." The idea is gradually to extend the clarity of mind, concentration, and absorption experienced in zazen to everyday activities.

The everyday activity to which I first attempted to apply right effort was taking a shower. Talk about your flow states! My approach to taking a Zen shower is a simple one; when showering, I shower, nothing extra. I try to become absorbed in my shower by paying attention to each detail. When I wash my face, I become conscious of each part of it. I'm aware of my eyes, then my nose, then my mouth, as my soapy hands glide over them. I feel the individual streams of water as they rinse the soap from my face.

As I wash, I become washing. There is no "I" doing the washing. There is no washing being done. There is only the activity of washing in which the water, soap, and man become one. When thoughts of I doing the washing enter my mind, I let them go. When thoughts of doing something other than showering pop into consciousness, I do not cling to them. I stay centered in the activity of the moment—showering.

There are many mornings when it is a great challenge to stay in the shower when I'm showering. My mind wanders to the events of the day ahead, jumps to memories of old friends, and gets stuck on things that would have been better left unsaid. I have to constantly remind myself not to follow these thoughts, and to get back to the task at hand, that is, the shower.

After even a few days of practicing right effort in the shower, you will notice some changes. They will not be dramatic changes. They will be subtle. You will find that your ability to keep your mind on your shower improves. You are less likely to catch yourself in full-blown fantasies or thoughts about other times and places. When you do, you can bring yourself back to the moment more easily. Your mind doesn't resist as much.

The reason that resistances to coming back to the moment diminish is because a subtle recognition and understanding are developing. You become convinced that the moment is the right place to be. A natural inclination to be in the moment, doing only what you are doing, begins to grow. You begin to feel mild discomfort when your mind is not in the present with your body, for example, when you're showering but thinking about the test you took last week or the one you have to take tomorrow. The realization that the only natural and proper place to be is where you are becomes more than words that appeal to the intellect for you. You start to feel comfortable in the moment, you settle into whatever you are doing, and you discover the simple but compelling joy of doing what life brings to be done in the moment. You become aware that the only reality is the moment. All else seems distant and artificial. All this happens one day when you *just shower*. Your shower becomes a form of water zazen.

You should try to extend right effort to as many of your daily activities as you can. I can tell you from personal experience that in addition to showering, washing dishes and other household chores, driving, walking, running, and other kinds of exercise are good candidates for your early attempts at applying right effort. Eating, when you're eating alone, of course, is also an opportunity for the practice of right effort. When you eat, just eat. Don't watch TV. Don't read the paper or listen to music. Don't think about anything, even eating. Just feel the texture of the food in your hands and mouth. Pay attention to each bite. Taste all the flavors. Consume your food, and be consumed by it.

You should gradually extend your practice of right effort to include everything you do. When all of your daily activities are done with right effort, you are truly living in the moment, doing what life brings to be done. Each activity becomes a unique experience to which you devote full attention for its own sake. Each task is done as a full and unique expression of you as you become each task.

In order to live fully in the moment or to do everything with right effort, you should consider each task an end in itself and become fully absorbed in each thing you do. One student's approach, which I have found useful, is contained in Christmas Humphreys's *Concentration and Meditation: A Manual of Mind Development*.

Begin by letting the whole of your day become an exercise in concentration, making each action to be done the one thing worth doing. First say to yourself: "I am now going to concentrate for (say) an hour on doing this, and let all other matters stand aside. This I shall do without thought of self, but because it is the right thing to be done." Then forget all about the need to concentrate and get on with the job, whether it be the passing of an examination, the drafting of a document or the cleaning of a room.

The practice of bowing, which is uncommon in Western culture, also helps you to pay full attention to the task of the moment. A bow before beginning a task symbolizes that you have deep respect for the task at hand and you intend to devote your full attention to it. When you bow, it means that you are putting all else behind you, and you are clearing your mind for the activity of the moment.

A bow at the end of a task is a way of clearing the mind and showing respect for the task you have just completed. You will find that if you approach each task with right effort, your bow will feel very natural. It will never feel forced or strained.

Just Studying

Just studying is what this book is all about. Just studying, like just sitting or just doing anything else, is the practice of right effort. It is an expression of the art of living through learning. It is doing with genuine effort what life brings to be done in the moment, when what needs doing is studying. It is the act of studying unself-consciously and with total concentration. It is harmony between you and your books; you are in step with the task. It is dancing with your books.

Studying with right effort is simply the application of the approach described for zazen to a learning task. The idea is to just study when you are studying, and not to do anything else. Many of the problems and pitfalls of zazen, for example, intrusive thoughts, are also associated with studying, and they should be handled the same way. Don't cling to them. Just let them go and get back to the task at hand.

In the beginning, the best way to approach studying, or any other schoolwork, is to resolve that you will sit for a specified period of time, say, an hour, and concentrate only on a specified task, say, reading a chapter of a textbook. The way to concentrate, as was previously pointed out, is not to furrow your brows and think so hard that your brain starts smoking. Concentration means that you simply let go of those thoughts, images, and desires that are keeping your mind from paying full attention to the task at hand. It means that you must be vigilant. You must first recognize that thoughts that are not relevant to your task, including thoughts of you doing the task, are intruding, and then let them go. Do not give them power by clinging or attaching to them. Promise yourself that no matter what comes up, you will let it go and return to the books. Even when you feel anxious and frustrated, just say, "Anxiety and frustration are here, I'll just let them go and get back to work." Or if you have an overwhelming desire, for example, for food when you have recently eaten, just say, "Desire is here, I'll just let it go and get back to my studying."

Sometimes during your early efforts at just studying, some imagery or visualization techniques can help. Imagine your mind as a light. It is a light that is always burning and linked to an unexpendable source of energy. To concentrate the light you must focus it on a single object and remove any particles in the path of the light that will disperse it. If you keep shifting the light from object to object, you will not see any one object very clearly. And if there are many small or a few large particles in the path of the light, not much light will reach the target object.

When your mind wanders from your studying and you start thinking about money, the pain in your side, or your inability to articulate your true feelings, visualize it as your mind's light straying from its target object. The way to get the light shining back on the proper object is not to jerk it and twist it until you force it to shine on the right place and keep it there. The best way is to simply and gently remove the other objects. Once the other objects are gone, your mind's light will naturally shine on the remaining object, that is, your books.

When intrusive thoughts interfere with your ability to concentrate on your studies, you can consider them particles that are dispersing your mind's light. Even if you could shine your light more brightly, it would not help. It would only illuminate the particles, and the target object would remain in the dark. It would be like switching on your car's high beams on a foggy night.

The way to deal with thought particles is just to let them go. You should not shine more light on them, that is, pay attention to them, because the more light you shine, the more they will absorb and disperse. And the last thing you want to do is stir them up. Their motion will disperse additional light. Just don't pay any attention to them, and they will settle and clear of their own accord. Just keep your mind's light focused on your books, and let the thought particles take care of themselves. As long as you don't focus on them or stir them up, they will clear. The central idea is that if you allow impediments and obstructions to fade into the background, you mind's light will shine fully on the task at hand.

Another image you can use is to consider yourself at the center of a spinning wheel. The center represents you doing what you should be doing in the moment, that is, studying. Here there is stability, calmness, and single-mindedness. As was mentioned earlier, there is only one center to a circle, but an increasing number of points as you move from the center. As you move from the center of the wheel not only does the area increase, the velocity of the spinning increases as well. If you move to the circumference, you could get thrown off the wheel.

The lesson to be learned is an obvious one. When you notice your thoughts moving away from the center of the wheel, let go and move back to the center. The way to do this is just to refocus on what you are supposed to be doing. Let go of the thoughts that are pulling you to the dangerous circumference, and you will naturally return to center, where the task of the moment awaits your full attention.

Your studying should become a practice of one-mindedness, like your zazen. You should not think of you and your books as separate entities. You and your books are a team. Together you are studying. You are working together, like dancers.

Approach your studies with an alert, unified, and calm mind. You should study as if you were put on this earth to do it. You're a natural. There is nothing else you would rather be doing. There is nothing else you can do in the moment.

You should be firm in your resolve that you are going to do a specified amount of work or work for a specified amount of time, no matter what. This kind of resolve takes much of the force out of intrusive thoughts as they arise, because you know you cannot act on them. For example, if thoughts of your friends or family come to mind that suggest some action, for example, a visit or phone call, the thoughts will not have much force, because you are already committed to not taking that action.

As your practice of just studying or studying with right effort ripens, you will notice that you can study longer with less effort. You will also notice that studying becomes less of a chore and more enjoyable. You might even begin to look forward to it, and begin to think of each study session as a journey in learning that is an end in itself. If you remain open and attentive, you will approach each trip with enthusiasm and freshness.

Part Three

MAINTAINING QUALITY AND ENTHUSIASM

Gumption Traps

Some of the most common problems that have been discussed in this book in relation to meditation and several others that are encountered in diagnosing and repairing mechanical problems have been called gumption traps by Robert Pirsig in *Zen and The Art of Motorcycle Maintenance*. *Gumption* is Pirsig's term for a down-home version of right effort. Gumption, according to Pirsig, is what a person experiences when he becomes wholly absorbed in what he is doing and there is no distinction between person and task. Gumption results from doing a quality job, the kind of job in which the doer doesn't obscure what is done. According to Pirsig, "The Greeks called it *enthousiasmos*, the root of 'enthusiasm,' which means literally 'filled with *theos*,' or God or Quality. . . . A person filled with gumption doesn't sit around dissipating and stewing about things. He's at the front of the train of his own awareness, watching to see what's up the track and meeting it when it comes. That's gumption."

Gumption is a Scottish word. It is a hearty word that smacks of cold mornings, thick porridge, and sheep in the glen. It means that you are aware of reality and embrace it. You do what needs to be done without sniveling, self-pity, or self-indulgence. When you have gumption, you meet the world on its terms in all its complexity and beauty. You don't go through life longing for some fantasy world. If the faucet drips, you fix it. You don't sit around wishing you knew more about plumbing or you lived in a world where faucets never drip.

The person with gumption approaches a task to be done with enthusiasm and an open, quiet mind. There is no rush. Whatever the task, he knows that he must stick with it until it is done, and he also knows that the doing is more important than what gets done. There is always more to be done. It is how you do it that really counts.

According to Pirsig, "a gumption trap ... can be defined as anything that causes one to lose sight of Quality, and thus lose one's enthusiasm for what one is doing." There are an infinite number of gumption traps.

There are gumption traps that are unique to a particular task or group of tasks. For example, Pirsig describes the out-of-sequence-reassembly gumption trap, which is a trap you can fall into when your task at hand is the assembly of a mechanical contraption, like a motorcycle. Pirsig points out:

> The first time you do any major job it seems as though the out-of-sequence-reassembly setback is your biggest worry. This occurs usually at a time when you think you're almost done. After days of work you finally have it all together except for: What's this? *A connecting-rod bearing liner?!* How could you have left *that* out? Oh Jesus, everything's got to come *apart* again! You can almost hear the gumption escaping. *Pssssssssssssssss.*

Other gumption traps described by Pirsig are pertinent to a wider variety of tasks. One class of gumption traps, called value traps, includes value rigidity, ego, anxiety, boredom, and impatience. These internal gumption traps, which are not directly linked to the nature of the task as is the out-of-sequence-reassembly trap, impede understanding and performance. They interfere with our ability to see things as they really are.

Most of these traps have been discussed before in

this book in terms of how they create time-place dissonance and interfere with right effort. In the next few sections, they will be discussed again from a gumption perspective, and suggested precautions and solutions will be presented.

Value Rigidity

Value rigidity and its cousin, conceptual rigidity, occur when your opinion and perspective preclude you from seeing things in a new light or appreciating something new. You are incapable of dropping your cherished view of the world or a part of it, and you reject anything that doesn't fit in with your view. Your cup is full, and you have no intention of emptying it to learn something new or different.

If you are value-rigid or in a conceptual bind, you have trouble seeing certain facts and relationships. The facts are there, but you refuse to remove the blinders that keep you from seeing them. Value and conceptual rigidity are the products of a closed mind. They are the antithesis of the open beginner's mind fostered in zazen. With beginner's mind, you enter a situation or approach a task without preconceptions. You're ready for anything because you're open to everything. Your mind is supple and alert. If, on the other hand, your mind is value-rigid, your approach is tense and brittle. Your mind is like a knuckle.

Pirsig presents the story of the old South Indian monkey trap as an illustration of value rigidity. The trap consists of a coconut or small box with a hole that is big enough for the monkey's open flexible hand to fit through, but is too small for his clenched fist. The trap is baited with rice, a banana, a cheeseburger deluxe, or any other food a monkey would find appealing, and the trap is fastened to a tree or stake. The monkey has no difficulty getting his hand into the trap. But once he grabs the food and forms a fist, he cannot get his hand out. The obvious solution is to let go of the food and slip out of the trap. The monkey, however, is so focused on the food that he doesn't let go. He cannot reassess the value of the food in light of his unexpected predicament. He values the food at all costs.

One way value and conceptual rigidity can interfere with learning is when students prejudge a course or a professor. In the department in which I teach, one of the most feared and hated courses is the required course in research methods and statistics. The course and those who teach it have undeservedly horrible reputations. Most students enter the course convinced that the course is designed so they can experience new dimensions in pain and anything they learn will be useless. Given the choice between root canal work and the course, most students would have a hard time deciding.

Not unsurprisingly, this course has the highest failure rate in the program. The problem is not the level of difficulty of the material. It really isn't that demanding. The problems in learning in this course are related to values and concepts. Because many students refuse to let go of the notion that the course is valueless and difficult, they don't give the course a chance. I've had students tell me, and I believe they are sincere, that they get so anxious they feel physically ill when they open the textbook for the course.

In the last few semesters, some of us who teach this course have started to devote more time to demonstrating the practical benefits of a working knowledge of methods and statistics and convincing students that statistical decision-making consists of the same process of inference that they use in their everyday lives. Our objective is to break the value and conceptual barriers so students will at least give the course a chance. In cases in which the students have let the the barriers down, they have invariably done better in the course.

The narrow-mindedness reflected in conceptual binds and value rigidity generally impede learning. They are especially troublesome, however, when the task at hand is problem-solving, because they limit the number and range of alternative solutions you consider. Since much learning is accomplished by problem-solving, especially if you are learning a particular skill or you are in a program, such as business administration, that uses a case study approach, it is important to recognize when you are caught in a value or conceptual bind.

A simple example will illustrate the importance of conceptual binds. Donald Schon, a philosopher turned management consultant, describes a situation in his book *Displacement of Concepts*: he was hired by a sandal-manufacturing concern to develop ways to increase its share of the sandal market as a response to declining sales. Schon's solution was to convince the executives of the firm that they were not in the sandal business, but in the leisure footwear business. By considering themselves only in the sandal business, a conceptual bind, they had unnecessarily limited their market. By expanding their concept of their business, they were free to enter markets they had never before considered. And they could expand their product line to sell in these markets without much change in their production process or distribution channels.

Many people are severely value-rigid when it comes to the examination of social problems. Their personal opinions about what causes or doesn't cause problems like poverty, crime, or teenage pregnancy limit their ability to investigate problems systematically, rationally, and thoroughly. They stick to their cherished conclusions about these problems despite evidence to the contrary and the development of new ways of looking at the problems. They refuse to let facts and logic interfere with their opinions.

Often, in the case of social problems, value rigidity promotes conceptual binds in problem-solving. It is not uncommon in our society to consider persons with certain kinds of problems as moral failures. If this view of the problem is rigidly held, the only solution that will come to mind to deal with the problems is to develop ways to deal with their immorality. Other solutions that are beyond the boundary of the narrowly conceptualized moral view of the problem will never be considered. To expand solutions, you have to expand conceptual boundaries. Sometimes the expansion of conceptual boundaries requires reducing value rigidity.

The first step in dealing with value rigidity and conceptual rigidity is awareness. When you read or hear something that sets off a mental alarm and you feel your mind start to knuckle up against it, try to relax and examine whatever it is without prejudging it. For example, don't go into your required philosophy course convinced that a bunch of ancient Greeks who thought the world was flat couldn't possibly have written anything relevant to your life. Go in with an empty mind. Go in without any expectations. Consider yourself a vacuum to be filled by what is presented in class.

Ego

The problem of ego has been discussed at length throughout this book. But since it is such a major impediment to right effort or doing a quality job, further discussion is warranted. Ego problems arise in many forms. One particularly offensive kind is arrogance. Here we have the Mr. and Ms. Know-it-alls of the world. There is really nothing they can be taught about a topic, and they are enrolled in a particular program, course, workshop, or training session only because it is a requirement to obtain a needed credential. This attitude just about guarantees that they will learn nothing. When egos are puffed up to this size, thoughts of self-importance take up all available mental space. There is no room for learning.

A less offensive version of the ego trap is related to value rigidity. As mentioned before, many students today attend college or take courses for strictly instrumental reasons. Their sole purpose is to improve their marketability. A course or information presented in a course that at first blush does not appear to have direct instrumental value is often discounted. If there is not a direct and obvious connection to enhancing students' attractiveness to potential employers, the information is considered valueless. Their only concern in taking courses is how can it make them look better.

Although there is nothing wrong with obtaining a college degree for instrumental reasons, there is something wrong with constantly worrying about how a course will make you look in the eyes of someone else. The problem is that you miss learning many things because you think they will do little to boost your stock in a certain market. There are two dangers here. First, you could be wrong about what will and will not improve your marketability. Students sometimes have misconceptions about what skills are needed on the job. For example, recently I was at a writing curriculum workshop attended by professors from a wide range of fields. A colleague from the business department told us that it is very difficult to convince her students that writing is important. Her students tell her that once they land jobs in the business world they will never have to write because they will have secretaries who will do all their writing for them. According to my colleague, who worked on Wall Street before entering academia, nothing could be further from the truth.

The second danger of this strictly instrumental approach to learning is that you limit your chances of experiencing the joy of learning. Real joy can only come from experiencing the thing as it is. It is the beauty of the poem. It is the elegance of a solution. There is a certain abandon to joy. The I is lost. To experience anything in terms of what it can do for you precludes experiencing the joy of it. Learn to learn. If it helps you get a job, great! If it doesn't, at least you can experience the joy of it.

Ego concerns destroy gumption in that they take your focus and enthusiasm from learning what is before you and redirect all your attention to you. You cannot possibly do a quality job under these circumstances. You can't get close enough to what you are supposed to learn, because you are in the way. When your ego gets too big, you become immobile and inflexible. If there isn't any room for anything other than your ego, how do you expect to learn anything? It's like cramming your room so full of pictures of yourself that you don't have any room for books.

Learning or doing a quality job on any task requires humility. You must be humble, open, and accepting. If you have an ego the size of a moose, you will not develop these characteristics. So an important step in learning to learn is to avoid falling into the ego trap by keeping your ego in check.

One exercise that you can try for reducing ego and increasing gumption is to practice taking "I" out of your conversation and thinking. The idea is that "I" gets between you and what you are doing so you become disconnected. Taking out "I" increases your "in" in that you become more involved and interested in what you are doing, and more in touch with your surroundings.

Think small when you start. Letting go of "I" for even a short time is very difficult. You have to be careful that you don't get "I" involved in diminishing "I," or you defeat the purpose of it. You can't become less self-centered and more task-centered by becoming egoistical about it.

Start with a half-hour a day. Each time you start thinking of yourself, each time "I" enters your consciousness, just label it an "I thought" and refocus your attention on what you are doing at the moment. This way you nip "I" in the bud before it grows to full bloom. If you let "I" thoughts grow unchecked, they take over the whole garden, and there is no room for anything else to grow.

A variation on the same exercise is to practice reducing ego while you are performing daily activities. This is the same as the previously described method of performing daily tasks, for example, showering, dishwashing, and bed-making with right effort. Try taking your drive, ride, or walk to school everyday without "I." You don't have to kick him or her out of the car or off the bus. Just don't pay any attention to him, and he'll leave of his own accord. Use the standard technique. First, recognize that you are thinking of "I" instead of driving or riding. This reduces the chance of "I" connecting with a bunch of other "I thoughts" and turning into a full-blown "I" episode or fantasy. Second, let "I" go. And third, return your full attention to what you are doing, that is, driving or riding.

A simple technique to help deal with "I" is to use a one-syllable word to replace the thought of "I" each time it arises. A word that has great meaning in Japanese Zen, mu, can serve this purpose. Each time "I" emerges, just say to yourself, "mu," as a way of deflecting thoughts of I and bringing your attention back to the activity of the moment.

The first thing you will notice when you start to deal with "I" is how difficult it is. You will notice that you think about yourself almost constantly, and soon after you recognize and let go of one "I," another pops, creeps, crashes, sneaks, cruises, struts, darts, worms, breaks, bursts, or bugaloos into consciousness. You will also notice how clever "I" is. "I" knows that if he can convince you that the way to forget "I" is to actively not think of "I," he has you. To not think of "I" is to think of "I." He also knows that when it is so hard to forget "I," you are susceptible to the following argument: "If a separate "I" doesn't exist and is unimportant or even harmful, then why does it seem so natural for you to think about "I" all the time?" The "I" who poses this question knows very well that for a person to be whole, to be a vibrant being, he must be part of the whole, connected to his environment. He must be so intimately involved in the process of give and take with his surroundings that there is no giver or taker. There is only being. There is only the person and the task as one in the act of doing. It is the doing that gives meaning to the self. To exist, a person must be intimately connected with his surroundings. There is no separate life. But "I" is selfish and deludes himself into thinking that he can exist apart from the rest. He can be just a taker. Let the givers give. Let the doing be for "I," not for the doing. Let thoughts of "I" fill your consciousness because "I" is the one. After "I," there is nothing.

Pursuing the way of "I" will eventually backfire. The more you think of "I" the more separate you become. You become more and more isolated. This is in direct opposition to the way the world operates. Everything is related. Yet you're operating as if you are not. How long do you think you can last in this unnatural state?

As your mind becomes more and more filled with thoughts of self, the distance builds between you and the world as it is. You live in a fantasy world in which you are the center. How sad. You're missing life and all its beauty. You're like the person who only talks about himself. The first-person pronoun is the mainstay of all his conversations. No matter what the topic of conversation, he somehow brings himself into the center. You stand before this person bleeding and in need of help. Instead of calling an ambulance, he starts telling you about the time he hemorrhaged and was almost lost to the world. It would have been such a pity.

You would think that someone would tell the self-centered conversationalist that by definition a conversation involves at least two people. How can someone learn about others or anything else if he only thinks and talks about himself? Doesn't anyone try to help him? Early on, they do. But after a while, people curtail or avoid contact with him, and he becomes either a social isolate or a person who has little intimacy in his life. He gets very little honest and caring response from people, and gets more and more out of touch with his surroundings, with social reality. After a while, he so out of touch that he doesn't know what he is missing. He completely loses contact. He lives alone.

When "I" dominates your thinking, you are out of contact with your surroundings. As you get better at your practice of paying attention to your drive or ride instead of thoughts of "I," you will notice all you have been missing. You see trees and buildings on your daily route that you never knew existed, you'll notice leaves floating in puddles, the way babies straddle their mother's hip, a spider's web, the smell of winter air, the human bustle of the morning rush. You'll begin to feel present and in touch with your surroundings. You'll feel that you are where you are supposed to be, which, of course, is where you are. Sometimes you'll wonder where "I" went. You'll chuckle and wonder how you could have thought that you couldn't live without "I." Then you'll realize that "I" is still there, but he's finally in the right place where he becomes just I.

This is not going to happen overnight. It will take dedication and constant practice. It is not going to be easy. When you first begin, expect a pretty hard time. The results will be discouraging. Sometimes you might feel a vague, general sensation of tension all through your body when you practice letting go of thoughts of "I." Just consider it the rumbling of the empty space left by "I" that will be filled by paying attention to the moment.

Anxiety

Anxiety, like ego, drains gumption, or separates you from the task at hand, because you are more concerned with how you look in the eyes of others than doing the job right. Once again, sense of self gets in the way. The difference between anxiety and ego gumption traps is that in the ego trap the person misses relevant information because he thinks he knows it all, whereas in the anxiety trap the person can't imagine himself not making mistakes and fulfills his own prophecy. Robert Pirsig describes the manifestation of anxiety in motorcycle repair in the paragraph following:

Anxiety, the next gumption trap, is sort of the opposite of ego. You're so sure you'll do everything wrong you're afraid to do anything at all. Often this, rather than "laziness," is the real reason you find it hard to get started. This gumption trap of anxiety, which results from overmotivation, can lead to all kinds of errors of excessive fussiness. You fix things that don't need fixing, and chase after imaginary ailments. You jump to wild conclusions and build all kinds of errors into the machine because of your own nervousness. These errors, when made, tend to confirm your original underestimation of yourself. This leads to more errors, which lead to more underestimation, in a self-stoking cycle.

Recognize anyone familiar in the above description? Sure, it's our old friend, the tormented Student Ego Monster. He either can't do anything or does it reluctantly because he is convinced that he will be a failure. He is unnerved by the thought of making a mistake because he equates errors with looking foolish. The correct view is that mistakes are opportunities for learning. We review what went wrong and right it.

The ego trap in which Professor M. Ego is caught and the anxiety trap that confines Student E. Monster are made of the same stuff. The victims of both traps get stuck on themselves. The difference is that M. Ego's primary concern is what the task can do for him, that is, how it can enhance his already lofty stature in the eyes of himself and others, whereas the major concern of E. Monster is what the task will do to him, that is, how it can destroy his already shaky self-esteem. In both cases, the problem is a focus on results or consequences instead of on the task itself. This focus impedes right effort by taking you out of the present moment and drains gumption by taking your attention away from the task.

One way to deal with anxiety and restore gumption is to limit your attention to the task itself. When you study, just study. Don't worry about how stupid you're going to look if you can't learn the material. You can hardly be enthusiastic about what you're studying or the paper you're writing if you dread the consequences.

How do you limit your attention to the task itself? Practice. Use the same techniques that you use in zazen, or use some imagery. When thoughts about what a jerk you're going to look like and how embarrassed you'll be when you fail enter your mind, just recognize them for what they are, let them go, and shine your mind's light back on what you're doing. When you feel yourself being pulled away from the center of the wheel by doubt and worry, bring yourself back to the center.

There are two areas of your educational experience where anxiety can be especially troublesome: asking questions in class, and taking tests. These areas deserve some special attention.

Reluctance to ask questions in class is often linked to fear of looking stupid. You are convinced that everyone else knows the answer to the question you are about to ask, and if you ask the question, the professor and your classmates will nominate you for the bonehead of the decade award, which is given every eleven years. So you sit silently and avoid disclosing your secret. You feel better knowing that no one will ever know you're a closet moron. That is until the test, of course, when the question you should have asked in class appears on the exam.

The practice of not asking questions that should be asked in lectures, seminars, and even informal study groups is gumption-destroying. Your enthusiasm for learning, the task at hand, is dampened by preoccupation with yourself. Real learning is the product of the liberation of creative forces. Enthusiasm requires a certain amount of abandon. You must be free of the constraints of egoism to become fully absorbed in learning. You have to jump in with both feet and hang the consequences. If you don't understand something, or if you want clarification or elaboration, ask questions. Even if you feel that you can't articulate it very well, ask anyway. Most professors who have been in the business a few years are pretty good at deciphering what you mean. Sometimes the professor or a fellow student merely restating your question is all that is needed for understanding.

Try asking a few questions without considering how you look. Think of it as an exercise to build gumption. You will see how truly liberating it is. Keep in mind, however, that you have no right to ask questions unless you have done all the necessary preparation for class.

Asking questions in class is not a burden that should be entirely borne by students. Professors must provide a classroom environment in which students want to ask questions. Autocratic, insecure, self-centered professors like Professor Monster Ego gleefully respond to questions that are either straw men for their favorite argument or shamefully supportive of it. Any question that threatens their position, however, is treated with disdain and places the questioner in jeopardy.

There are also professors who are ill-equipped to answer questions because they have not approached their jobs with right effort. These are the teachers and researchers who have not thought about the problems and issues in their fields or read an article in a scholarly journal since they received their degrees. They are woefully unprepared to teach a course, and they have been droning out the same lectures for years. Such professors are not very receptive to questions, because they can't answer them. If you really feel full of gumption, ask the question anyway. Maybe it will help some professors realize that it is time to put some gumption in their teaching.

There are many approaches to making students feel less self-conscious about asking questions. My pal, Chris Zimmerman, a professor at Indiana University of Pennsylvania, has students complete a feedback form after each class session. In addition to asking students to rate his effectiveness in delivering the specific lecture, he requests that they anonymously write on the form any questions they have about the lecture or the associated readings. At the beginning of the next class session, he addresses their questions.

One idea for promoting the asking of questions that was put into practice in one of my courses was to wear zany hats. The rationale was that there wasn't any question students could ask that could make them look more ridiculous than they already looked in their goofy lids. They had nothing to lose by firing away. The course in which I tried the idea was an introductory applied statistics course. So our hats were called stat hats. The hats came in all shapes and sizes. One student wore a papier-mâché duck on her head for the entire semester; another wore a different hat for every class. We had a lot of fun with our stat hats, and it is my impression that they went a long way in getting students out from behind their faces so they could ask questions.

I'm not suggesting by this example that professors should introduce gimmicks to sell their courses like car dealers hawking the latest model. I am suggesting that both professors and students think of ways to increase the number of quality questions asked in a course. Good questions are a sign of gumption. They indicate that students are involved and enthusiastic. Professors who are teaching with right effort will devise ways to elicit good questions, and the ways should be appropriate for the nature of the subject, the professor's personality, and the students enrolled in the course. Stat hats are not for everyone. But methods for reducing anxiety about asking questions are a good idea for most courses.

Tests are the other major cause of anxiety among students. Heart pounding, hands sweating, nerves racing out of control, you pick up your pen to answer question one, but then nothing comes. "Where did all the information go?" you cry. "Memory, don't fail me now." But you sit there in a state of shock, while the test goes on. Sound familiar? It does to many students who are victims of test anxiety, a kind of performance anxiety that ranges from mild tension to complete immobilization.

One of the best ways to deal with test anxiety is to prepare well for the examination and have confidence in your preparation. Start studying early for the test, and study with right effort. Enter the test without a doubt in your mind that you did everything you could to get ready. Have confidence in your preparation. Know there is nothing more you could have done. All that remains is to take the test with right effort and gumption. Become fully absorbed in the test. If all the while you are taking the test you are thinking that you should have studied more or better or you're wishing the test was over, you are not in touch with the task at hand. As you do in zazen and your other practices, keep bringing your mind back to what you are supposed to be doing.

Do a few minutes of zazen before the test if you get a chance. One kind of zazen that seems particularly appropriate is called kinhin, or walking zazen. There are various ways to do kinhin, usually after a period of sitting zazen. Since your pre-exam kinhin may be within sight of others, you will want to be as inconspicuous as you can. So just walk at your normal gait and count exhalations, just as you do in sitting zazen. Follow the same instructions as for sitting zazen, except for the hand and leg positions, of course, and meditate in motion for a few minutes.

If during the exam or while studying for the exam you feel a sudden surge of anxiety, try the following exercise. Take a deep breath through the nose, using your diaphragm, and fill your lungs to their full capacity. As you feel the air draw in, think of it as a fresh, calming stream coming into your body. As you expel air through your mouth, think of it as the anxiety leaving your body. Repeat the exercise five or more times.

This exercise is known as "cleansing breath." It is described by Bo Lozoff in *We're All Doing Time*, which is a book of spiritual advice and practices for prison inmates. If this technique can help prisoners deal with the fear and anxiety of doing time in a maximum-security prison, it should do wonders for test anxiety.

Some students are very superstitious about tests. They have rituals and charms that include lucky meals, shirts, pens, and seats. These are all pretty harmless, and in some cases they are useful because they reduce test anxiety. However, one kind of irrational belief increases anxiety. Some unfortunate students are superstitious about test anxiety.

There are people who feel that if they don't suffer a certain level of test anxiety, they will fail the examination. These are the same people who always publicly predict they failed the test because to say otherwise means certain failure. In other words, they claim failure as a way of increasing their chances of success. You can't get any more irrational than that. These students are convinced that unless they experience considerable torment before, during, and after the examination, they will not and do not deserve to do well.

This kind of anxiety caused by superstition has the same basis as all other forms of anxiety. The problem stems from emphasizing results instead of the task at hand. These students think that in addition to studying they can influence results by worrying. The solution is simple. Concentrate on what you are doing, and hang the consequence. If you don't have results on your mind all the time, there is nothing to worry about. When thoughts like "If I think I'll do well, I will definitely flunk" enter your mind, just let them go, and get back to the task at hand.

What if you don't do very well or actually fail? Do you just disregard it because it is a result? No. It is now a fact in the present. It is something that has to be accepted and dealt with. It is now time to review to see where you went wrong. Was it in the way you studied for the test? Did you answer a question that wasn't asked? Did you spend too much time on one question? Did you have lapses in concentration while studying or taking the test?

You should not feel ashamed or sorry for yourself. Let those feelings go like all others. Pick yourself up. Dust yourself off. And get back in the game. Mistakes are part of life. If you don't make them you're not living in the real world. You're living a sheltered life in which there are no challenges or risks. The questions is not whether you will fail. Everyone does sometimes. The question is how you handle it.

If you act with right effort, there are no failures. Consequences do not matter in terms of success or failure. They matter only in terms of what needs to be done next in life. If you bake bread and it rises, then you bake it and eat it. If it doesn't rise, then you see where you went wrong, and you start over.

Gumption is sticking with something despite initial failure. The only kind of failure that matters is quitting. There is no failure in trying again with sincere and genuine effort, even if you try a thousand times. It is the trying that is important, not the results.

A sure way to fall into the anxiety gumption trap is to worry about progress. There are both short-term and long-term versions of this trap. The short-term version will be discussed in "Impatience," page 105. The long-term version of the progress trap is to worry constantly about how much closer to some goal each activity is bringing you and constantly evaluate your performance in relation to the goal. This is a problem of time-place dissonance. There is an overemphasis on goals at the expense of process. The difficulty is that if all your attention is on results, on accomplishing a certain objective, you can't possibly pay attention to what you are supposed to be doing in the moment to contribute to accomplishing that objective.

A subclass of progress problems emerges when your goal is personal growth of some kind. I think learning to dance with your books or study with right effort and gumption falls under this rubric. One problem that can occur when you are trying to study with right effort is that all the time you are studying you're evaluating how right your effort is. The difficulty is, of course, that instead of studying with right effort, you are thinking of right effort. They are not the same. To study with right effort, you just study. Thoughts of right effort are like any other thoughts; if you cling to them they take you away from the task of the moment.

It seems paradoxical, but you will not be able to study with right effort if you concentrate on right effort. If you are humming along with right effort, as soon as you think right effort or congratulate yourself on your gumption, it will vanish, kaput! You can see, then, that you will be in for a rough time of it if you are checking the rightness of your effort all the time.

Progress, in most cases, will be gradual. If you expect sudden inspiration and bursts of learning, you will be disappointed and frustrated. Although you will become more inspired in your work and your performance will improve, it will not happen all at once.

The best way to avoid disappointment and frustration is simply to concentrate on what you are doing in the moment and let go of thoughts of progress. You must be patient and have confidence in the method. You must convince yourself that staying centered in the moment is the best way of doing things.

Beginnings are especially anxious times. You may find the going rough during your initial application of right effort to schoolwork. Although right effort is effortless effort, it takes persistence and patience to achieve. You may feel that you will never get it right when you first try it. Disturbing thoughts will constantly drag you away from your studies, and you might feel hopeless and overwhelmed. If an hour of studying with right effort presents such difficulties, a lifetime of doing everything with right effort and gumption might seem out of the question. You feel that you will never be able to sustain your effort.

The way to stem this initial anxiety is to back off, slow down, and take one step at a time. Thinking about a lifetime of total concentration when you first start to practice is like imagining a lifetime without cigarettes or chocolate when you're trying to quit. A lifetime without cigarettes seems hopeless. One day, hour, or minute, however, is manageable. As the days accumulate into years without cigarettes, you become more and more comfortable without them. You finally reach a point at which it is hard to believe that you ever smoked. You can't imagine how you lived that way for so many years.

The key to the practice of right effort is to do it a moment at a time. Don't get ahead of the moment. If you start thinking about the rest of your life, you'll get overwhelmed. All you should expect of yourself is to try to do what you are doing at the moment with all the gumption you can muster. Bo Lozoff offers some solid advice on taking one moment at a time: "Find various ways to remind yourself . . . of the fact that the real work is just one moment at a time. If we had to make huge changes up front, none of us would ever see the Light. Big change is just a bunch of little ones."

Another source of anxiety is comparing your progress with that of others. Always comparing yourself with others will interfere with your concentration. Comparisons are dangerous because they take you away from what you are doing in the moment, can be discouraging if you don't measure up to others, and can inflate your ego if you do better than others. As we have seen again and again, all three possibilities destroy gumption.

If your attention is truly centered on process, as it should be, and not on results or progress, you will not be tempted to make comparisons. The experience of learning and discovery is what is most important. There will always be more to learn, no matter how advanced you become or how well you do. The key to continual learning is to realize the importance of process, to learn as well as you can what you are currently studying, and to avoid comparisons.

This does not mean that you cannot learn from others. It often helps to observe and talk with those who are doing well. The techniques they use may help you with your studies. There is nothing wrong with comparing techniques and approaches and experimenting with them. The trouble starts when you compare people and apply "superior" and "inferior" labels.

Comparisons can be especially destructive to your gumption when you conclude that you're not smart enough or quick enough ever to really understand. Forget about being smart enough and quick enough. You are you. Accept that your smartness and quickness are within a certain range, and approach the experience of learning with your smartness and quickness. You can't approach it with anyone else's anyway.

Boredom

I subscribe to the theory that there are no boring subjects, there are only bored students. If this were not the case, you would not find so much variation in how interesting you find any one subject. Anyone who has studied a subject for any period of time knows that it can be at times fascinating, at other times deathly dull. Since the subject does not change that much, it must be the person.

Boredom means that you have lost your beginner's mind. When you're bored everything is stale and monotonous. You no longer see each moment as a unique event. You no longer consider each moment a once-in-a-lifetime opportunity to do with right effort whatever needs to be done. You are no longer fully absorbed in what you are doing.

Simply take a break when you find yourself bored. Return to the task after you have had some sleep, a cup of coffee, or some entertainment. Keep in mind, however, that boredom that doesn't respond to a break, or chronic boredom, can be a symptom of serious gumption problems.

Chronic boredom means it is time for a right effort check. You may have let yourself slip into your old habit of just going through the motions when you study. You're no longer fully involved, and you let thoughts of other things and places rescue you from what you now see as the drudgery of schoolwork. It is time to get back on track. Take some time to meditate. Then reaffirm your commitment to study with right effort and take one moment at a time. Study for short periods of time, taking breaks between them, until your gumption reservoir refills. Sometimes, even when your gumption is at full power, you should count a few breaths between chapters or assignments as a way of maintaining your gumption.

You should build breaks and recreation periods into your daily schedule as a way of avoiding boredom. Occasionally, you should schedule a "big break"—a day or even an entire weekend. Keep in mind, however, that moderation is the key to returning refreshed from the "big break." If your break becomes a "lost weekend," your break will be degenerative instead of restorative. In other words, don't act like a Shaltoonian.

Those of you who are familiar with Kilgore Trout's (a.k.a. Philip Jose Farmer) epic science fiction saga, *Venus on the Half-shell*, will recall that the Space Wanderer, Simon Wagstaff, an Earthman who travels through the universe with an atomic-powered banjo, a female robot, an owl, and a dog, spends a short time on Shaltoon, a planet on which there is ancestor rotation.

Each Shaltoonian is made up of cells that contain the memories of all of his ancestors. Once a Shaltoonian reaches puberty, his body is taken over by one of these ancestors each day of the week, except one. Shaltoonian years are twice as long as earth years and the life expectancy of a Shaltoonian is two thousand years. This means that the more dominant ancestors (cells containing ancestor memories compete to take over the body) will appear at least once during a person's lifetime.

As a result of ancestor rotation, Shaltoon never advanced beyond a simple agricultural society. The reason that ancestor rotation and progress are incompatible is obvious. When an ancestor takes over the body, he is not about to spend his day working on labor-saving devices, plans to restructure the economy, or a philosophical treatise on the rights of the host body. Although the ancestor is expected to do some work to ensure that society continues, a large part of his day is spent in the frenzied pursuit of the fulfillment of carnal desires. On most days, the planet of Shaltoon is a huge fleshpot, and very little gets done.

Each ancestor, when given his opportunity, eats, drinks, and copulates with wild abandon. The majority of the population on any one day is rocking out in the fast lane. The order of the day, every day, is to consume compulsively at a frenetic pace. Life is an orgy.

Sounds pretty good, huh? But somebody has to pay the piper. Consider the poor person who inhabits the body the morning after, which is every day. As everyone who has spent too much time in the fast lane will tell you, eventually it catches up with you. On any given day, a large proportion of Shaltoonians are incapacitated by the excesses of their ancestors. As Kilgore Trout describes it, "Every once in a while, the body would collapse and be carried off to a hospital by drunken ambulance attendants and turned over to drunken nurses and doctors. The poor devil who had possession that day was too sick to do anything but lie in bed, groaning and cursing. The thought that he was wasting his precious and rare day in convalescence from somebody else's fun made him even sicker."

It is bad enough when somebody else does this to you, but imagine how you'll feel if you lose a day because of your own excesses. Don't kid yourself. Everyone feels guilty and stupid when they can't get on with their daily routine because of the aftereffects of excessive consumption of food, drugs, or alcohol. No matter how you try to redefine it by using one of the stock sayings, like "if you don't feel bad the morning after, you haven't had a good time the night before," a hangover is a hangover is a hangover. Don't let your "big break" break you. Practice moderation.

A close relative of the boredom trap is the energy, or interest, trap. Here you wonder when you begin a task if you will have enough steam to make it through. Your concern is that sometime during the performance of the task, such as writing a paper, your energy and interest will dissipate to the point where you're bored, tired, and frustrated. You're afraid that somewhere during the completion of the project your initial enthusiasm and resolve to do a quality job will turn to drudgery and exhaustion. What's the sense of even starting? Why not wait until some other time when you know you have the energy and the attendant interest to carry you through?

The energy trap, although directly linked to a concern about boredom, is also related to the anxiety trap. Your concern is that you do not have what it takes to complete the job. You feel that you are wanting in essential resources, that is, energy and interest. And you convince yourself that while you may currently have the energy and interest to start the project, it will quickly be drained, and you will be left flat and enervated. The thought of eventually reaching this point makes you so tense and anxious that you postpone starting the task.

The problem that creates the energy trap is a lack of confidence. You are unsure of your ability to sustain the level of energy and interest needed to do the job. There are two recommended approaches for avoiding this trap. The first you already know well by now. It is to forget about you and your shortcomings and get on with the job. Let go of those self-centered thoughts about what you can and can't do, and just do as best you can what needs to be done in the moment. Invest yourself and spend yourself entirely in what you are doing at the moment. Don't worry about running out of energy. Sink into whatever needs doing. Get totally absorbed in it. Don't make the mistake of checking your feelings to see if you should begin a project or continue one. Don't ask for emotional permission to go ahead by inquiring about your reserves of energy and motivation. If you do, you will constantly be concerned about running out. Questions about your energy, interest, and motivation levels will breed thoughts of doubt. These will take your thoughts away from the present and the task at hand.

The second approach is to build your confidence in your store of energy by realizing it is limitless. You have all the energy in the universe at your disposal, if you realize that you are one with the universe. Techniques for tapping into the universal source of energy, known as *ki* in Japanese, are commonly taught in martial arts—judo, kendo, archery, karate, and akido. A similar concept, *drala,* is part of the Tibetan Shambhala.

One technique for tapping into the limitless source of energy is to imagine as you breathe in that you inhale the energy of the universe into your body and mind. Let it surge through you. Feel its power. Let each cell absorb its regenerative force. You are restored. Refreshed.

Imagine as you breathe out that you exhale your boredom and other problems. You are expanding into the universe to share in its infinite energy. Feel secure in knowing that universal energy is available to you. This should have a calming effect, which in turn makes more energy available to you. You don't waste energy in anxiety and worry about its availability when you are sure of a plentiful source. You actually conserve energy through your confidence in the universal supply. You no longer squander your energy resources by worrying about them or trying to push yourself through boredom.

Impatience

You are most likely to fall into the impatience trap when you underestimate how long a job will take to complete. Unanticipated problems are common when working on just about anything, and unless you are prepared to deal with them, you can become frustrated and angry when you encounter them. These emotions can, of course, deplete your gumption supply.

You should give yourself plenty of time to do a job, and plan a modest amount of work. It is a mistake to think that you can overhaul an entire engine, paint a house, or write a research paper in one day. Some impatience, frustration, and anxiety can be avoided if you break down the job into manageable parts and give yourself enough time to complete each of them without rushing.

One kind of impatience trap is a short-term version of the progress trap. It occurs when you constantly worry about how long it is taking you to complete a single task. For instance, you have three chapters to study for an exam, and while you are reading the first chapter you're watching the clock wondering if you will have time to finish all three before the test. You feel rushed and wish you were further along. After each page of chapter one, you turn to the end to see how many more pages you have to go.

You whiz through chapter one, consuming words but not digesting them. You finally finish. And . . . horrors! It's chapter two. How much more can you take? If chapter one was the introductory chapter, the one that always takes it easy on you, and it took you an hour to read it, chapter two will surely take you the rest of the night to read. It's hopeless. Give it up. Why put yourself through this frustration?

The cause of this impatience is twofold: you did not allocate enough time for studying; and you're thinking about results, that is, finishing all the chapters, instead of process, that is, understanding what you are reading at the moment. A good general rule is to estimate realistically the amount of time it will take you to finish an assignment or study for an exam, then double it. This gives you enough time to deal with the unanticipated problems that always arise.

If you give yourself enough time, you will not feel pressed for time, and time and progress will not be on your mind so much. You will be much less likely to become frantic or feel hopeless. Finishing will not loom so large in your mind, and you will be better able to concentrate on what you're doing. You might even enjoy it.

Setting aside enough time so thinking about time does not interfere with your performance requires planning and self-discipline. It is a good idea to have a monthly calendar on which you record significant dates, such as due dates for assignments and exam dates. Then you can plan your daily activities around these dates. If your plan is realistic and you stick to it, it can go a long way in reducing the anxiety caused by time-place dissonance or worrying about finishing when you should be concentrating on what you're doing.

A daily schedule can be a great help in reducing anxiety. If you follow one, you don't have to make a decision about what to do next each time you complete a task. There is no question about what you are going to do next—just look at your schedule. But in order to benefit from a schedule, you have to follow it pretty strictly. If it's time to study your least favorite subject for two hours, study your least favorite subject for two hours. Don't kid yourself into thinking that it's probably more important for you to go for a tension-reducing mile swim than it is to study because you wouldn't get anything out of studying when you're so uptight. Don't trick yourself into thinking that you will do a double study session the following day. Just stick to the schedule.

You should, of course, build into your schedule ample time for meditation, leisure, and exercise. And you should avoid falling into the trap of worrying all the time about being on schedule. In this trap, your whole day is a frantic effort to get everything on your list done. As you're doing one thing, for example, a reading assignment, you're wondering if you will finish in time for your scheduled workout. While you're working out, you're constantly concerned that you won't get to the laundry.

How do you avoid becoming a slave of your own making by shackling yourself to a schedule that destroys your gumption and keeps you in a constant state of time-place dissonance? First, you should be realistic. Don't try to do too many things in one day, and give yourself enough time to complete each activity on your schedule. Second, each day when you write your schedule, reaffirm your commitment to do each task with right effort. Get yourself in the right frame of mind before you start each task. It sounds hokey, but say to yourself before each task, "For the next X hours, I am going to do Y with full concentration. I will be fully absorbed in Y. My whole world will be Y. When thoughts other than Y come into consciousness, I will let them pass and get back to Y."

There will be days when you have to alter your schedule. Don't worry about it. But make sure that you have a good reason for doing it. Never postpone a task you don't feel like doing because you think you'll feel more like doing it some other time. Put aside your feelings, and get on with what needs to be done.

If you must prune your schedule, use some rational criteria. Drop those activities that are not essential to meeting the nearest due date on your monthly calendar. If you find, however, that every day you are eliminating the same routine activities, for example, meditation, exercise, and calling your mother, it is time for some self-examination.

Keeping calendars and schedules is essential for students with jobs or other important responsibilities, such as children. These planning devices can help to ensure that you judiciously allocate your valuable time so you pay adequate attention to all areas of your life.

Expansion

Techniques for restoring gumption and avoiding pitfalls have been presented throughout the discussion of internal gumption traps. Several additional techniques for restoring gumption or approaches to conserving gumption are pertinent to all internal gumption traps. One technique, which was alluded to in the discussion of the energy trap, is known as expansion, and it can be used when gumption traps are encountered or as a preventive technique to ensure against gumption depletion.

All the gumption traps that have been discussed produce subject-object bifurcation or person-task separation. They create barriers between you and the task at hand, and build resistance to learning. Gumption traps are deep, dark holes in which you are confined. They keep you from seeing the light of knowledge. They limit and constrain. The opening of the hole becomes smaller and smaller the longer you remain in it. Eventually, you are cut off from the rest of the world.

Loss of gumption results in psychological contraction. Your attention becomes directed inward. You become narrowly focused on yourself. You wrongly assume that by paying more attention to yourself, you can soothe those ragged edges and jangled nerves, comfort your bruised ego, and restore the desire to learn. The reality is that when you circle your psychological wagons to protect yourself, you keep out the rest of the world. The result of this contraction away from the world and into yourself is that you become hard, brittle, constricted, and impermeable. These are hardly conditions that promote learning.

Learning requires expansion. You must reach out, open up, and let in the material to be learned. You must let down your barriers, expand your boundaries, and accept new information. You have to crawl out of the hole you have dug for yourself and see the light. You must merge the self into the task or the task into the self and dissolve the person-task separation.

The notion of expansion is central to Zen. Enlightenment occurs when awareness or consciousness expands to include everything and the boundaries between the self and the world completely dissolve. One approach to attaining this state is known as the internalization of the external. When you come to the realization that everything you thought was happening outside you is actually happening within you, you have internalized the external. This means that the world does not exist outside you. Everything happens within your interior space. Everything that happens to you is part of you because it happens within you.

Christmas Humphreys considers the realization of all-encompassing internal space a powerful force, and he sees its expansion as important for dealing with all kinds of events. He suggests that we consider ourselves vacuums that contain an infinite amount of space. By expanding our internal space to infinity, we have plenty of room to accommodate within everything that happens in our world. By accepting what were formerly thought of as external events and circumstances, we gain an unprecedented sense of control. Even negative events lose their power to unsettle, anger, and frustrate when they are accepted as part of our internal space.

The notion of expansion of internal space can be useful in developing techniques for dealing with the psychological contraction or reduction of space for learning and working that occurs with the depletion of gumption. The first step is to think of internal gumption traps as contractions. Imagine that your internal space resides at some location in your body, for example, just below the navel, between your eyes, or where the tip of your tongue touches the roof of your mouth. When you encounter a gumption trap, for example, anxiety, during studying, allow yourself to feel what it is doing to your internal space. You should feel contraction or a shrinking sensation in the area where you have located your space.

Once you feel the shrinking, visualize your anxiety as a belt tightening around your internal space. Allow it to get tighter and tighter, and then, POP. Your internal space suddenly expands beyond the boundaries of the belt and encompasses it. Your space is no longer bounded by the belt, that is, your anxiety, but the belt has been absorbed into your internal space. The belt of anxiety no longer controls the space, but your internal space surrounds the belt.

What happens when you successfully use expansion techniques to escape internal gumption traps is that you accept the gumption trap as part of doing the task. The task and the trap are seen as part of your internal landscape. They are not something external to you that must be shaped, pushed, prodded, cut, or blocked. You have expanded your internal space to include them, and like everything else within you, they are just there. They must be accepted. To deny them is to deny reality. They are just as much a part of you as your age and eye color. Let them enter your vacuum or infinite internal space, and get on with the task at hand. Let them dissipate in the infinite space within.

Expansion techniques are useful not only as a method of gumption renewal or restoration but also as a preventive measure to avoid gumption traps. One technique is to approach any task, for example, studying for a test, by imagining your internal space, once you have located it, expanding until the task itself and everything associated with the task, such as anxiety about not finishing in time, are part of your internal space. They reside within you. You can look within and actually see everything there, including yourself working on the task.

Once the task is within your internal space, imagine the space occupied by the task as work space. Further imagine that the task will remain in the work space until it is completed. You cannot work on anything else in that space until you finish the task. The task is part of you. The space and the task are inseparable, and the space is your internal space, not something outside of you.

Visualizing the boundaries of the self expanding and imagining yourself as a vacuum are expansion techniques that are relevant to all the situations you encounter in your life. For this reason, you should practice them even when you are not faced with a stressful situation or a difficult task. Try to experience all things as if they were happening inside you. Be open, flexible, permeable, and accepting. Practice increasing your internal space every day. Start by locating your space and visualizing it as the size of a pea. Gradually allow the space to expand. Let it grow to an immense size. Soon it will grow so large that there will be no space between you and other people, ideas, and situations. Everything will take place within one huge space. Expand your awareness to the limit. Swallow the universe. Gulp!

Bagging

A technique that has been suggested for people who suffer from worry and anxiety is to designate one period of their day, for an hour or so, to worry. During that hour, they can worry about anything that comes to mind. At other times of the day, however, they are instructed not to allow themselves to worry. They must postpone worrying until the designated hour.

A similar technique could be used to extract yourself successfully from internal gumption traps. Set aside half an hour to an hour each day for indulging yourself. Get as egoistical as you like. Become shamelessly arrogant, bored, petulant, frustrated, angry, anxious, scared, helpless, hopeless, or worried. Grovel, snivel, and whine all you want. Be a spoiled brat. Act as if you're the only one in the world who has ever felt pain. Maybe you could even have a good cry. Scream. Rant about how unjust the world is to you.

When you encounter any feelings that are associated with gumption depletion at a time other than the designated emotional hour, set those feelings aside. Promise yourself that you will re-create the feeling during the proper time, when you will give it your full attention. It might help to imagine that you are putting the feeling into a bag. When the designated hour arrives, you open the bag and let the feeling out.

You will find when you open your emotional bag at the designated emotional hour that your feelings have lost much of their force. Indeed, some may seem absolutely silly when they are no longer closely tied to their original context. If, however, they were allowed to attach to the original event rather than being put aside, they would have interfered with your studying. For example, if you become anxious when you are studying for a test, and instead of bagging your anxiety you let it take over, you could become immobilized by the emotion.

Don't confuse bagging with suppression of emotions. You are not bottling up your feelings. You are recognizing your feelings, and letting them go into the bag. You are putting aside your feelings. You are not holding back.

After you have been bagging your feelings and opening the bag at the designated hour for a while, try burning the bag instead of opening it. Take a quick inventory of all the emotions you have in the bag, and then just imagine the bag being consumed by flames. If you need something more concrete, you might try writing down the problems, thoughts, and feelings that interfere with your work throughout the day, dropping them in a paper bag, and putting a match to it when the designated time arrives.

Relaxation

The best body-mind state for effective performance of just about anything is alert relaxation. In this state, you are aware of your environment, including the task at hand, and you have the mental flexibility necessary to respond to changes in your environment. You are in the flow because you are part of the environment. You are in touch with the task at hand and with your surroundings.

Anxiety, boredom, and other emotions and mind states that produce tension are contractions that impede flow and create distance between you and your environment. You become uptight and rigid. You lose the openness and flexibility that are necessary to recognize changes and respond to them. As the tension increases, your awareness narrows. Your attention becomes centered on your uptightness instead of on the task at hand and your work environment. There is no joy in your work. There is no rightness in your effort. You become impatient. The tension amplifies. You stop working. You give up. But the tension remains. And now it's tinged with guilt. Your neck is tied in knots. You feel the tension in your shoulders and back. There is pressure in your head. Your body cries out for relief.

You're in luck. There are hundreds of techniques that have been practiced for centuries as methods for reducing tension and producing relaxation. These techniques restore the gumption destroyed by tension because they produce the flexibility and openness required to get in touch with your surroundings. They help you dissolve the barriers between you and your books that are created by tension. Relaxation techniques can go a long way in getting you back into the flow of studying.

One of my favorite techniques has been described by Joel Levey in *The Fine Arts of Relaxation, Concentration, and Meditation: Ancient Skills For Modern Minds.* I suggest that you use this method, or others you may discover, any time you feel an uncomfortable amount of tension before or during studying. By uncomfortable I mean when you feel so tense that it interferes with your studying or you feel tension-related pain in your back, neck, head, stomach, or shoulders. In his book, Joel Levey provides the following instructions for Rainbow Light Relaxation:

Begin by sitting comfortably, with your spine straight, your eyes soft, jaw loose and body relaxed.

Now vividly imagine that you are surrounded by a luminous mist of relaxation and well-being. Mentally give this mist a red color [or any other color that works for you] and a warm comforting emotional feeling. Next, begin a cycle of five deep and slow breaths. As you inhale this relaxing mist and hold the breath for a slow count of five, imagine it filling your head, neck and shoulders and soaking deeply into every pore and fiber of your head, neck, and shoulders. As you breathe out, imagine exhaling all of your physical tensions, thoughts, cares, or mental dullness that may be stored in this region of your body. Imagine exhaling any physical, emotional or mental disease as smoke or fog being flushed completely out of your body by this luminous relaxing mist. Imagine this fog or smoke dissolving completely into the space around you.

With a second cycle of five breaths, focus upon your

torso including your hands and arms. Vividly imagine and feel this relaxing mist flowing in through your nostrils, filling the center of your chest and then spreading out throughout your hands, arms and torso, filling this region completely with a luminous, warm, relaxing feeling of red mist and light. As before, hold the first breath for a slow count of five, allowing the oxygen to saturate and nourish your tissues and wash away the waste products from your muscles and brain. Vividly imagine this entire region is now alive with a vitalizing red glow of deep relaxation.

With a third cycle of five breaths, direct you attention to your lower body including your hips, buttocks, genitals, legs and feet. As you inhale, vividly imagine this luminous relaxing mist flowing down to your navel and as you exhale imagine it diffusing to completely fill the whole lower portion of your body. Allow the following breaths to find their own natural rhythms and depth. Vividly sense and imagine this entire region of your body aglow with a deep soothing sense of relaxation, warmth and vitality.

With a last cycle of five breaths, vividly imagine that you are breathing in a pure crystalline mist and rainbow-like light. Allow the waves of the breath to come and flow effortlessly at their own natural rhythm. Imagine that this luminous substance flows first to the center of your chest and then pours forth throughout your whole body. Direct this powerful purifying and harmonizing light to any region of your body that is out of balance and which calls for healing. Sense and deeply feel that your whole being is now pure and clear like a crystal body which is flooded by rainbow light. . . .

Once you are familiar with this basic technique, you will be able to access the same results with only four breaths: with the image of red light draw in one breath to fill and cleanse your head and neck, one breath to the torso, one to the lower body and a fourth breath to flood your whole crystal clear body with rainbow light. With further practice, you will be able to master this method with a single breath by simply super-charging your whole mindbody with a rainbow-like relaxation at any time or place that you wish.

You should either use a tape recording of the instructions for rainbow light relaxation or have a friend read them to you when you first begin to practice the technique. You will quickly learn the instructions by heart; this will allow you to use the technique anywhere at any time. You can even use it when you become tense during an examination.

The 95-MPH Cornball Pitch

No matter how I try to say it, the message I will try to convey in this section sounds corny. Yet, it is a powerful message that is consistently found in various forms in self-improvement and inspirational literature. The message is "love yourself."

Loving yourself does not mean self-love. It does not mean you should become vain and self-centered. Indeed, it means that you become less focused on yourself. Loving yourself means self-acceptance. It means being comfortable with yourself. Once you allow yourself to be you, which is what you were intended to be, you don't have to try to be anyone anymore. Being you doesn't require any effort. You're supposed to be you. It's natural for you to be you. You don't have to work at it. You don't have to pay attention to you. You can just be what is.

Loving yourself requires that you accept whatever has happened in your past and what you are, think, and feel in the present. If you are anxious, love yourself for being anxious, and get on with the task at hand. Don't resist. Accept whatever you are at the moment. There is no need to dwell on it.

Some people are terrified by the thought of just being themselves. They can't find much to like in themselves, and they are convinced that if they were just themselves, other people wouldn't like them. They often feel unworthy and undeserving. They may even be victims of self-hate who never allow their real self to break through a formidable facade of their own construction. Maintaining the facade requires a great deal of energy that could be better spent doing what needs to be done in the moment.

Whenever you start to feel the "uns"—unworthy, un-wholesome, uninspired, and/or unloved—take a minute to relax by counting a few breaths. Reflect for a moment on the thought that you must accept whatever you were in the past and you have a duty to try to do your best in the present. This is the most that you or anyone else should expect of you.

Daily Affirmations

One way to start the day with gumption is to recite a list of affirmations that reflect the behaviors and attitudes required to carry out your day with right effort. Recitations of the basic tenets of a philosophy or approach to life are commonly heard in groups, programs, and organizations that are devoted to personal growth. For example, in some karate dojos, training sessions begin and/or end with a spirited group recitation of principles by which one should train and live one's life—for example, train earnestly with creativity; be humble and polite; do not be too proud or modest; be calm and swift; live a plain life.

You can develop your own set of statements to reflect the principles by which you want to conduct your life. By reciting them each morning, you reaffirm your commitment to live by your principles. Here is one short set of reminders that I have found helpful.

1. Accept events and circumstances.
2. Live in the present.
3. Don't take things personally.
4. Accept the past.
5. Don't dwell on yourself.
6. Let go.

7. Don't worry about personal gain.
8. Do not speak out of anger.
9. Do not criticize others.
10. Do everything with right effort.

Lists of statements that contain important principles are not only useful at the beginning of your day but can be used throughout the day when you notice that your gumption supply is getting low. Whenever you feel your enthusiasm wane or your involvement in the moment diminish, take a break and review your list.

Short inspirational quotations from your favorite authors can also be used to help restore gumption. Keep a small notebook in which some of your favorite passages are copied, and refer to them when you feel the need.

The Study Group

Group support has long been recognized as an effective way to promote and maintain value, attitude, and behavior change. During World War II, Kurt Lewin, a German social psychologist who emigrated to the United States, demonstrated, through a series of controlled studies, the importance of the group as a vehicle for change. Lewin's studies provide scientific support for what has been done in Zen monasteries for thousands of years. Traditionally, group meditation has been an important part of Zen practice.

Many structured, repetitive activities that require considerable discipline are performed by groups of people. Not only are many forms of meditation done in groups, but aerobic exercise, dance, and martial arts are also typically practiced in a group setting. The group provides support, companionship, and advice. It promotes the values and attitudes that are needed to sustain effort through the hard times. It provides a forum for discussion and exchange of information.

The study group is hardly a novel idea. The kind of group that will be suggested in this section, however, differs from the traditional study group. Most students who study in groups study the same subject before an examination, and their conversations usually center on the content of what is studied. The book-dancing study group I envision is a group of students who meet on a regular basis to study a variety of subjects. Discussions would center on the process of study rather the content of study. Group meetings or book dances could even include short periods of zazen at the beginning and end of the sessions, and kinhin or walking meditation could be used as a study break. The meetings might even include some dancing. In some sesshins, which are meditation retreats that last for several days, participants do some free-style dancing, which makes everyone look pretty silly, as a way of letting go of ego. It seems the theory behind the dancing is that it is hard to maintain the fiction of self-importance when you are doing a ridiculous dance.

The exact practices that are followed by a group will depend on its composition. At a minimum, members should agree to meet at the same time at least four days a week. Meetings should last at least two hours. Silence should be maintained during study and meditation. Discussions about the process of study should occur after the study session, and they should not be counted as part of study time.

One group activity that might prove useful to members is to discuss at the beginning of the week one suggestion or technique presented in this book. Each group member would try to put the technique into practice during the week. Insights, problems, and discoveries related to putting the technique into practice could be discussed for a short time, say ten or twenty minutes, at the end of each study session. Once all members feel that they have improved their understanding of the technique and refined its application to their studies to the point where they are comfortable with it and are benefiting from it, it is time to go on to a new technique or suggestion.

Missing a book dance or study session is a very serious matter. The absence of any group member can undermine the commitment of fellow members and drain gumption. Members should consider participation a sacred duty. Joining a group should not be done as a lark. It is a serious commitment.

One way to promote commitment is to establish a group identity through, for example, giving your study group a name, for example, the Douglass College Book Ballet and Hot Fudge Company. Or you could perform group rituals at each meeting as a method of reaffirming your commitment to the group and to studying with right effort. Here I am not suggesting that you sacrifice small mammals, eat peyote buttons, or chug a gallon of wine coolers before each study session. Chanting a set of affirmations or performing a group dance is about as ritualistic as you should get.

The number of persons who can attend a book dance is not limited. Book-dancing groups can range from small troupes to large companies. As long as everyone abides by the fundamental rules of attendance and silence during meditation and study periods, space is the only limitation on the size of the book dance. Who knows, a few years from now, we may find entire auditoriums at some schools filled every evening from seven to eleven with book dancers. Book dances for entire colleges may be held during exam weeks! Students might even travel to other schools to attend book dances.

Although participation in a group generally increases gumption or enthusiasm for an activity, there are dangers associated with group membership. One peril is that group meetings can degenerate into gripe sessions. Unproductive whining and complaining can undermine the very purpose of the study group. Group meetings under these conditions will result in gumption depletion instead of gumption promotion.

This is not to say that group discussions should not focus on problems. They should. But the discussion should be about concrete problems of studying that are defined in such a way that potential solutions emerge from the discussion and can be explored. Save your bitching, which is more a style of interacting than of problem-solving, for the cafeteria or rathskeller. Keep study group discussion focused on problems of study techniques and behaviors related to academic performance.

A second peril of study groups is group egoism. Although group identity is important for establishing commitment to proper study habits, if members of the group start to think of themselves as something special because they are members of the group, they will run into all the previously discussed problems of ego. Remember, the purpose of the group is to help you study with less ego, not more.

Part Four

NUTS AND BOLTS: REQUISITE SKILLS

Skillful Means

The first three parts of this book have stressed techniques for promoting the right attitude toward studying. The emphasis has been on developing the appropriate frame of mind for studying with right effort. Studying, it has been argued, is not some unnatural act that should be dreaded and avoided. It is natural to use our brains, and if we use them correctly by giving our full attention to the task at hand, studying can be effortless and enjoyable. Getting to the point of effortless effort or flow, however, takes commitment, discipline, and patience.

The importance of doing anything you do with right effort cannot be exaggerated. Effective studying, however, requires something in addition to right effort. You also must develop good studying techniques and skills. You must learn proper methods for reading a textbook, taking a test, writing a paper, and managing your time. Entire manuals have been written on each of these topics. This part of the book will provide you with some simple suggestions in each of these areas for developing the rudimentary skills necessary for effective performance in school.

Those of you who already have good study habits and well-developed skills can read through this part of the book quickly. For the most part, it will merely confirm what you already know and do.

For others, this part of the book will contain relatively new and valuable information. Some of you are unaware, for example, that there are systems for effective reading of textbooks. You will find that putting some of the suggestions that follow into practice will make you a more efficient and effective student.

For still others, the suggestions in this book may not be enough. You may need basic work in some subjects, for example, mathematics or English, in addition to improving your studying skills. If you think you need help in any area, don't wallow in self-pity, resentment, or embarrassment—march over to your school's remedial, tutorial, or learning center, and sign up. Most colleges have such programs where you can get individual help or take a noncredit course.

Some of skills and knowledge that are essential to your education are not discussed in this book. Every student should know his or her way around the library and have basic computer skills. The best way to acquire the necessary skills is to contact the library and computer center at your school and find out what they have to offer. Often libraries offer educational tours and lectures about using special collections. Most computer centers offer minicourses, free or for a nominal fee, on personal computers and the use of packaged programs on mainframe computers. You will not believe how much easier your life will be when you know how to use the library and a computer.

Assessment

The first step in changing anything, from your tennis swing to your study habits, is to find out what you are doing or where you are now. Once you identify your present position, you can move in the direction in which you want to go.

There are two general approaches to self-study or self-assessment of your study habits. The first approach is retrospective. You take account of what you do, including how often and how well you do it, by reviewing your past. You rely on your memory to provide the details required to conduct the review.

The obvious dangers of this approach are memory decay and distortion.

A more accurate and useful approach to generating the data needed for self-assessment is to keep a diary of your activities. Select a typical week of school and record everything you do, starting with what time you get up each morning and ending with what time you go to bed each night. Include everything—meals, job, class, recreation, shower, conversation, chores, everything. Use a notebook as your daily activities log. Carry it with you, and record activities on the spot. Don't trust your memory by waiting until the end of the day to record all your activities.

Entering a few descriptive column headings on a fresh page of your notebook each day will serve as your daily log. The headings for most routine activities, such as meals, work, recreation, and meditation, will simply indicate the nature of the activity and how much time you spent doing it. Whenever the activity is schoolwork, a few additional pieces of information should be recorded. An example of a log appears in Figure 2.

Figure 2   *An Example of a Daily Log*

Date: 11/8/89

Out of bed: 8 A.M.

In bed: Midnight

Activity	Start	End /	What	Why	Where	How Well
Shower and personal hygiene	8	8:20				
Meditation	8:20	8:40				
Breakfast	8:40	9:00				
English class	9:00	10:30				

Activity	Start	End /	What	Why	Where	How Well
Study	10:30	11:30	French—Translation Exercise 4	Overdue assignment	Library	6
Study	11:30	1:30	Math—Reading and note-taking/ Text Chs. 5–6.	Prep. for next week's test	Library	4
Lunch	1:30	2:00				
Math class	2:00	3:30				
Read novel	3:30	4:00				
Soc class	4:00	5:30				
Workout	5:30	6:30				
Dinner	6:30	7:00				
Job	7:00	10:00				
Study	10:00	11:00	Chem—Reading and note-taking/ ½ Ch. 5	Assignment for next class		
TV & talk w/ roommate	11:00	12:00				

As shown here, keeping a daily log requires that you simply note the time you started and finished for most activities. The information recorded when the activity is studying is more involved. What you studied should include: the topic (for example, history) and the specific tasks you accomplished, for example read pages 12–50 of text, solved problems 1–3, answered questions 4, 7, and 9 of chapter 1, wrote three pages of a book report, or reviewed class notes.

Why you studied should reflect your specific purpose for studying, such as keeping up with assigned reading, writing a paper that is due next week, or studying for today's test.

How well you worked is recorded in the last column. Here you should rate yourself on a ten-point scale from 1 (very poorly) to 10 (very well). Base your rating on the quality of your concentration and how much you accomplished in the time you spent working. If, for example, you read one page of a history textbook in an hour and you spent much of the hour daydreaming, you neither concentrated effectively nor worked efficiently. Your rating should be 1.

Keeping an activities diary is a chore. There is no denying it. It is intrusive and tedious. But it is necessary if you want to improve your study habits. And you will find that it gets easier as the week progresses.

After you have spent a full week (seven days) making entries in your diary, you should conduct an analysis of your activities. You can start by aggregating or summarizing the information over the days the diary was kept. The purpose of aggregating or summarizing is to answer important questions about how you spend your time.

The first step in aggregation is to develop a set of general categories that reflect routine activities in which you should be involved. Some examples of categories are sleeping, eating, exercising, studying, working at your job, meditating, and attending classes. An example of a summary sheet is provided in Figure 3. When you reduce the information in your diary to this form, you will clearly see how you have been spending your time.

It should be clear from the example above that the student used for Figure 3 is not the same productive and conscientious student used in Figure 2. Our student whose weekly activities are presented in Figure 3, Mr. Soporific S. Slug, provides a fine example of a misspent life. Mr. Slug is spending two-thirds of the hours available to him in a week either in bed or

Figure 3 An Example of an Activities Summary Sheet

Activity	Number of Hours
Work	20
Studying	7
Class	15
Exercise	0
Meditation	0
Household and personal chores	6
Social recreation (watching TV with friends)	20
Solitary recreation (watching TV alone)	20
Eating	10
Sleeping	70

watching television. He devoted 110 hours to these two activities during the week he kept his diary.

A glance a Slug's summary form should tell him that he needs to redistribute his available time among his activities. His specific objective should be to spend more hours a week studying and to spend less time sleeping and watching television. Slug should develop and implement a specific plan or set of activities to achieve his goal. For example, he should make a commitment to reduce his television watching by at least half, and to allocate the reclaimed time to study, exercise, and meditation. Gradually, he should reduce his television time more and more, and spend his time in more productive and satisfying ways.

Slug should make his transition from videophile to solid student in stages. One way to guarantee failure is to try to change everything at once. It is unrealistic to think that radical change will be lasting. Slug should set realistic and manageable goals. For example, during his first week he should try to reduce his television watching by two or three hours and increase his study time by an equivalent amount. Once he has accomplished this, he will have the self-confidence to reduce television watching by the same amount the second week and to reallocate the time to other activities, such as study, exercise, and meditation. In about twelve weeks, Slug will have his television watching within reasonable limits, and he can start working on his sleeping.

A review of Soporific S. Slug's activities summary sheet has indicated that he is not spending enough time on schoolwork in relation to his other activities, especially television watching and sleep. Problems like Slug's of not giving enough time and importance to schoolwork have been recognized by Dr. Luis Neives of the Educational Testing Service as one of the two typical study problems. The other problem is ineffective study. This problem arises when you put in the time but you don't get much out of it. In other words, you are trying but not learning. The big danger here is that you conclude that you are not capable of learning, and you give up. In most instances, the problem is not that you are incapable of learning, the problem is that you don't know how to study.

How do you know how effectively you have been studying? There are two sources of information on your effectiveness. One is external review. That is your professors' evaluation of your performance—your grades and professors' comments on your work. The second source is a review of your activities diary with specific attention to studying. You can develop a summary sheet for your study activities, but in most cases, a visual inspection of your study activities entries in your diary should tell you how well you are doing, and it should give you some clues as to what you are doing wrong.

You have recorded in your diary a rating of the quality of your concentration and how much you accomplished for each study period. The computation of an average rating will give you a global rating of your effectiveness. To calculate an average rating: (1) multiply the rating for each study session by the number of hours studied to the session; (2) add together these weighted ratings; and (3) divide this sum by the total number of hours studied. The following formula represents a summary of the procedure:

$$R = \frac{\Sigma\,(hi)\,(\gamma i)}{\Sigma\,hi}$$

where
R = average rating per hour of studying
Σ = sum
hi = hours studied for individual session
γi = rating for individual session.

Below is the computation of R for the student whose activities appear in Figure 2:

$$\frac{(1 \times 6) + (2 \times 4) + (1 \times 5)}{1 + 2 + 1} = \frac{19}{4} = 4.75$$

If your average rating is low, for example, 3, you are not studying effectively, and you should take some corrective steps. A first step might be to review some additional information. For example, inspect the column in your diary that indicates where you study. If your investigation indicates that you consistently do your schoolwork in places like bed, sauna, and hot tub, perhaps a change in study environment is needed.

An inspection of your diary entries may show that you do fine when you study some subjects but not others. This may indicate that you should work on your approach to or attitude toward those subjects you are studying ineffectively. Further inspection could show that they are your most difficult subjects, and you usually study them late at night, after you have finished working on your favorite subjects. If this is the case, obviously, you should move them up in your study plan. Study the subjects with which you are having the most difficulty when you are fresh.

If the ratings of your study effectiveness are uniformly low, it is time to renew your commitment to studying with right effort, and you should reread the pertinent sections of this book. Review the quality of your effort. Are you letting irrelevant thoughts carry you away from your books? Are you in the past or future instead of in the present? Are you worrying about results and consequences at the expense of fully involving yourself in the activity of the moment?

One of the most telling questions you can ask yourself in relation to your studying effectiveness is "Do I know the correct way to read a textbook?" Since about three-fourths of the time you spend on schoolwork is spent reading, you're in trouble if you don't know how to do it right.

Reading

Most of the reading you will do as a college student is studying assigned textbooks for courses. Textbooks, as a thousand people before me have said, should not be read like novels. Although reading a textbook may be pleasurable, reading a textbook is not the same as reading for pleasure, that is, diversion or recreation.

Many students, even good ones, do not know how to read a textbook. They read inefficiently because they read passively, without a question or purpose in mind. Several methods or systems have been developed to help students become more active, involved, and efficient readers. One of the earliest, widely used, and best-researched methods was developed by Professor Francis Robinson and tested at Ohio State University. Robinson's SQ3R (Survey, Question, Read, Recite, Review) method is based on the findings of educational research, and the method's effectiveness has been demonstrated in studies of college students.

SQ3R represents a system of five steps for reading an assigned text.

Step 1. Survey

In this first step, you take no more than a couple of minutes to scan the headings in the chapter you are about to read and read the summary or conclusion of the chapter, if one is available. The purpose of the survey step is to orient you to what you will be reading. It informs you of the main business of the chapter and the author's purpose in writing the chapter. The survey provides you with an idea of the main points that will be covered and the scope of the chapter. In sum, the survey furnishes you with a preliminary sketch of the structure and content of the chapter, and it is a first step in preparing your mind to accept and retain the information presented in the chapter.

Step 2. Question

Now you actually begin reading the chapter. You start by turning the first heading into a question that directs your reading. Reading with a question in mind is active reading. As you read, you are looking for an answer to your question. Your reading is directed by the question, and it helps to organize both the information in the section you are studying and your thoughts about the information. This kind of active or involved reading will increase your interest, comprehension, and retention.

You do not have to spend a great deal of time formulating the question that will direct your reading of a section of a chapter. In most cases, it only takes a few seconds to convert the section heading provided by the author into a question. For example, if you encountered "Fear of Crime Among the Elderly" as the heading of a section of a chapter, your question might be simply "How afraid of crime are the elderly?" Sound simple? It is. More important, it is also effective.

Step 3. Read

Once you have posed your initial question, read to answer that question. Do not be at all surprised if new questions emerge as you read. Typically, reading to answer one question generates others. It is these questions that will give form and relevance to your reading. They will make your studying more interesting and memorable.

Step 4. Recite

After you have finished actively reading a section, briefly state in your own words the answer to your questions. If you cannot answer your questions, review the section for pertinent information.

It is a good idea, at this juncture, to jot down some brief notes that outline your answers and capture the main points of the section. Robinson calls these notes "working notes" to distinguish them from the extensive verbatim notes many students take while they read. The criteria for working notes are that they must be brief and written (1) only after the section has been read, (2) from memory, and (3) in your own words.

Nieves refers to notes as "self-talk." He recommends that everyone develop a system of note-taking that suits his or her individual needs, but in general, notes should be organized around these three questions:

1. *What are the key words and phrases defining the subject?* These words and phrases are usually used as headings and subheadings and are words that must be known.
2. *What are the facts, definitions, and events to be remembered?* These are the main body of the notes; they are to be understood in a general sense but not memorized.
3. *What are your thoughts, reactions, and reflections?* These reflect what you understood at the time of making the notes.

Nieves suggests that you divide your notebook page (or pages if you write across two pages to give yourself more room) into three columns by using the headings "Key Words," "Facts, Definitions, and Events," and "Thoughts and Reactions." He also suggests that you review your notes shortly after you write them, and clarify and reorganize them during the review.

Many authors object to taking notes verbatim from the text. I do not, if it is done sparingly and judiciously. Often authors will write a couple of sentences that make the point of a section of a chapter in a cogent, pithy, and memorable way. It is permissible to copy it into your notes as long as you also briefly state it in your own words.

When you are reading for a research paper, it is entirely proper to copy quotes from sources. Quotes are often used in papers to lend authority to a point or argument; to preserve subtle, powerful, or beautiful language that makes a point that would be lost by paraphrasing; to document a general point with a specific illustration; or to present information in a cogent way that cannot be improved upon. Care should be taken, however, in note-taking for a paper that you do not fall into the trap of copying the majority of your notes from your readings. To avoid this trap, follow this simple rule: before you copy directly from a source, state your purpose for copying the quote, and write the meaning of the quote in your own words.

Step 5. Review

One way to minimize memory decay is to place the material you have studied firmly in your mind by reviewing it. The review should be conducted after you have finished reading the entire chapter. The primary materials to be reviewed are your working notes on each section of the chapter. If your notes have been done right, they should provide both an outline of the main points in the chapter and answers to the questions you posed while reading the chapter.

Reviewing is actually a form of recitation. After you

have reviewed your notes, place them aside and try to recall the questions and answers that guided your reading and the main points of the chapter. Then review your notes to see how well you retained the information. If something is not clear in your notes, return to that section of the chapter to clarify the point. Revise your working notes if needed.

The main purpose of using a system of study like SQ3R is to help you become an active reader. It is important to become involved with what you are studying. Otherwise, you read passively and ritualistically.

How many times have you come snoring to the conclusion of an assigned reading without having any idea what it was about? If someone asked you to list the main points of the chapter, you would answer them with the old moon face. Sure you read the chapter. But you read it ritualistically. You just went through the motions. You read it because it was assigned, and you were supposed to read it. Maybe you even felt some satisfaction when you checked it off your list of things to do. You accomplished something. But what did you really accomplish? Nothing that you can recall very clearly!

Reading by the SQ3R method is an aid to studying with right effort. The method helps to keep what you are supposed to be doing in the moment clearly in view. If you are actively questioning while you read, you are less likely to drift off to places in the mind other than the present and to think about doing things other than the task at hand—that is, comprehending and retaining assigned reading materials. Methods like SQ3R help to keep you firmly centered in the task of studying when what life brings you in the moment is something to study.

One characteristic that the SQ3R method shares with right effort is that it may not be easy to apply to your studying at first. Like anything else, you have to practice it before you get good at it, and when you first try it, you feel awkward and inefficient. Don't get discouraged. Or if you do, let it go, and keep practicing SQ3R with right effort. After a while, it will become second nature, and you will be studying at peak efficiency.

There are a few special topics or applications of SQ3R that deserve brief attention. The first is underlining. Don't get me wrong. Underlining itself is not necessarily bad. It is the way that many students underline that causes problems. I speak from experience. I won't bore you with the painful details of the complete confessions of a compulsive underliner. I will simply state that I used to underline everything. Not only that, I sometimes underlined everything in more than one color. The inefficiency of underlining everything or almost everything in a chapter is obvious.

Although underlining poses many dangers and taking "working notes" is preferable, underlining can be part of an effective approach to studying if it is done in the context of the SQ3R method. Francis Robinson's suggestions for incorporating underlining into the SQ3R method, to be found in greater detail in his book *Effective Study*, are:

1. Survey the headings and summaries quickly to get a notion of what major points will be covered.
2. Turn each heading into a question as you start to read that section.
3. Read the section to answer the question.
4. Recite your answer to the question first by thinking what is important and then finding the phrase or phrases that briefly state this point. Be careful not to underline more than a phrase cue, and use a marking system that shows the degree of importance of each point.
5. After reading the entire lesson in this manner review your "outline" of underlinings to get a picture of what the chapter has been about, and recite again to fix these ideas in mind.

Remember to wait until after you have read the entire section before you underline; underline only important points; and think about the relevance of what you are underlining. If you add a few working notes in the margin of the text, the effectiveness of underlining as a study method can be greatly enhanced.

Supplementary or collateral readings are sometimes assigned in addition to the text for a course. These readings are often assigned or suggested because (1) they expand on important areas covered in the text, (2) cover important areas that the text does not cover, or (3) present an opposing or different viewpoint to that presented in the text or in lectures. Often supplementary readings are not textbooks, and their organization and structure differ from a text. For example, you may find that there are no headings to turn into questions when reading some essays, or you might find that the headings are more literary devices than descriptions of the content of the section. Nevertheless, the SQ3R method can be applied to supplementary reading.

The survey step, according to Robinson, is designed to orient you to the book, essay, or article. Here you determine why the book was assigned and examine the preface, forward, and chapter headings, if they exist. Once you have a clear idea of why you are reading the material and the general structure and content of the material, you can take the next step and start posing questions that will be answered in step 3, reading.

Normally, for supplementary reading you read for a longer period than you read in a textbook before you reach step 4, recitation. Indeed, it is sometimes possible to read several chapters, especially if the supplementary reading is a novel, before you stop reading to relate the material to the questions you have posed. The one question you should always keep in mind while reading supplementary material is "How does this material relate to the main thrust of this course, or, why am I reading this material?" During the recitation step, take some working notes that you will later review as the final step.

As a student, you will be faced with the task of reading articles in scholarly or professional journals, sometimes in preparation for writing a paper. Some journals assist with your reading of articles in that they have a standard format authors are required to follow. For example, articles on empirical studies in the social and natural sciences usually have sections on the research question or hypothesis, methods, findings, and significance of findings or conclusion. You will find these headings used so consistently that you can develop a form for your working notes that can be used to summarize the content of similar articles. Each form will feature questions that correspond to the standard headings, and you can simply write your notes in the appropriate place after you finish each section. As part of your working notes, you should indicate correspondence and divergence between studies. By the time you have read a substantial number of studies in an area, you will have a good idea of the scope of questions, methods, and findings, and you will have much of the information needed to write your paper.

When reading for a paper, a review to commit material to memory is not crucial. Your fifth step should be to review and relate. Your objective in reviewing should be to relate the main points of the article you have read to other articles and to the outline of your paper. Your question in reviewing should be "Where does this material fit in with everything else I have read and the structure of my paper?" The next section presents a fuller discussion of this topic.

Writing

This section deals with the kind of writing that is most important to most academic careers, that is, writing reports and term or research papers. This kind of writing is usually a matter of (1) asking the right question, (2) gathering the information that is needed to answer the question, (3) evaluating the merit of the information, and (4) drawing a conclusion. These four steps are relevant to a wide range of writing tasks. For example, it does not matter if the source of your information is scientific research findings or personal introspection; you still have to judge the weight of the evidence in relation to your question.

There are three keys to writing good reports and papers: (1) clarity, (2) Clarity, and (3) CLARITY. Although many people delight in ambiguity and try to dignify confusion, such qualities have no place in good report writing. Even when you are trying to convey ambiguity, you must do it in an unambiguous manner.

This does not mean that you have to have everything thought through completely before you begin to write. Writing and thinking are not separate processes where one precedes the other. Indeed, writing is a form of thinking. Often we don't know exactly what we think until we try to get it down on paper. Our thoughts about a topic really take shape when we start writing.

You should not expect your first stab or draft of a paper to be completely polished and clear. These are the objectives you desire to achieve over several drafts. Your first draft is a way to see what you know, what you need to find out, and what direction your thoughts on the topic are taking. Howard S. Becker, a famous sociologist who teaches a writing seminar for graduate students at Northwestern University, recommends that your initial draft of a paper be a free write. After you have immersed yourself in the literature on a topic for a while, sit down and write what is on your mind. Don't worry about spelling, the rules of grammar, or organization. Just write. Don't edit while you write. Don't evaluate. Just let it flow.

The first draft is a working draft. Review it to see what central themes and ideas emerge from it, and to see if there is some organization scheme or structure embedded in your initial written thoughts. Note where more information is needed, where ideas need to be clarified or fleshed out, and where language needs to be polished. When you're ready, write the second draft, and continue the process of creating (writing) and evaluating (editing) until the paper seems right to you.

A misconception held by many students is that good writers sit down and knock out a final version of a piece at their first sitting. Students have this notion that writing more than one draft is an indication of a lack of talent. Nothing could be further from the truth. Good writers write and rewrite and rewrite and rewrite. Writing is not only an art and a talent but also a skill and a discipline. Writing is not the invocation of creative muses while in a state of torment, joy, or intoxication, as some would have us believe. It is work. Hard work. It requires diligence, persistence, and patience.

The two rules that apply to studying, meditating, and anything else you want to do proficiently apply to writing: (1) begin, and (2) continue. Practice writing every day. There are certainly enough opportunities for daily writing while you are a student. Write when you are happy. Write when you are sad. If you let your feelings dictate when you write, you will never write a sentence.

There are two deadly traps to avoid when you write: (1) sesquipedalian prose, and (2) personal opinions that are not documented with appropriate evidence or sound logic. You fall into the first trap when you follow the thesaurus school of writing where you find the longest words you can to express your thoughts. For example, you write, "homo sapiens who reside in crystalline shelters should refrain from catapulting geological specimens," when writing, "people who live in glass houses shouldn't throw stones" would have made the point much more simply and clearly. This does not mean that you should always write in simple declarative sentences and use words of no more than two syllables. You should do what it takes to express your thoughts in the clearest and most interesting way.

The second trap is just as dangerous and irritating as the first. It will guarantee you a low grade on a research paper with any professor worth her or his salt. Unsubstantiated opinions have no place in research papers. For example, if you are writing a research paper on the death penalty, and you happen to be a proponent of it, you should avoid making statements like "murderers should be executed because they are killers." Not only is this tautological or circular reasoning, but it is also a statement of your preference for what we should do with murderers without any support for your opinion. Statements like "we should kill killers because they are slime bags" and "we should kill them because they turn my stomach" are equally out of place. Your opinions, statements, and conclusions in a research paper should be based on principle, reason, and fact. If you are writing a paper about capital punishment, you should be familiar, for example, with arguments, pro and con, based on philosophy of punishment and the empirical evidence on deterrence.

There are dozens of manuals and guides on how to write a research paper. One that I have used is Dean Memering's *Research Writing: A Complete Guide to Research Papers*. Memering suggests that the development of a research paper can be considered a process of five steps:

1. Select a General Topic Area.
2. Do some preliminary reading.
3. Frame your question or thesis.
4. Begin collecting your data.
5. Finish collecting data, and write your paper.

Step 1. Select a General Subject Area

In this step, you select a general topic that you think is interesting and important within the framework of the course for which you are writing the paper. Often the chapter headings in your text for the course can provide you with some general areas, or your professor will suggest areas for you. Interesting topics are often mentioned in lectures or included in your assigned readings. For example, while reading for a course about social problems you become interested in suicide.

Step 2. Begin Preliminary Reading

In this step, you begin to familiarize yourself with the literature in the area you have selected. You learn what issues are currently important in the area, what questions have been answered, and what questions remain to be answered.

Your preliminary reading introduces you to the language and concepts that have currency in the area you have selected and provides you with the context within which your research question will be posed. Preliminary reading is the first step in framing your research question. You should keep an open mind while reading, and let the literature lead you to your question.

In this step, your reading should be fairly general. If your interest is in suicide as a social problem, you should be reading broadly based book chapters on suicide as a social problem and reviewing articles on suicide in the social problems periodicals. Examining the reference section or bibliography of the book chapters you have read should lead you to relevant journal articles.

At this juncture, your objective is to educate yourself generally about the problem. Who commits suicide? Where? When? What are some of the common explanations for the problem? Is it on the increase?

Step 3. Framing the Question

Your question should emerge from your preliminary reading. After you have become familiar with the general literature in an area, you should start to gravitate to topics that seem especially interesting or important to you. This is where your question will come from. For example, while doing some preliminary reading on your topic, suicide, you become interested in suicide in institutions. After further reading, you become interested in suicide in penal institutions, especially municipal lockups and county jails.

If in your reading, you find that some experts claim that lockups and jails have a comparatively high suicide rate because of the kinds of people they confine. Others claim the high rate is attributable to the harshness of the penal environment. You have your question.

In posing your question, you should keep in mind that you are not writing a general interest piece for a popular magazine. You are posing a serious, interesting, worthwhile question. Memering's guidelines for a good question or thesis are that it should be specific, limited in scope, worthwhile, and researchable—that is, there should be enough understandable published information available for you to answer your question.

Asking the right question is very important. The question shapes your investigation and therefore affects the quality of your answer or solution. Be creative in your questioning. You must ask new questions to get new answers. Sometimes you have to break conceptual bonds or look at problems in a new way to obtain new solutions.

Step 4. Start Collecting Your Data

Now you begin reading specifically to answer your question. If your question concerns the contribution of personal and environmental factors to suicide in jails and lockups, you would start by gathering all the literature you can find on the topic. References like the *Criminal Justice Abstracts* and the *Psychological Abstracts* would be useful in locating articles on this topic. Other services that could be useful in locating information on a variety of topics are *Dissertation Abstracts International* (DAI) and *The Education Resources Information Center* (ERIC). It is possible to conduct computer searches for many abstracting and indexing services. One of the best ways to conduct a computer search is to use the DIALOG/Information Retrieval Service. It stores in excess of two hundred abstracting services and contains over thirty-five million entries. Ask your librarian about using these services.

You should keep an open mind as you read and collect information to answer your question. Additional information could lead to a more important or interesting question. Or you may find that you have to modify your question because your reading indicates that it does not meet all the criteria of a good question. For example, if you found that there were very few articles on suicide in jail but many on attempted suicide and other forms of self-injury in jail, you might expand your question and make it more researchable by broadening it.

Step 5. Finish Collecting Data and Write the Paper

After you have written the initial draft of your paper, a general outline should emerge. If you have followed the steps suggested by Memering, the general format for your outline already exists. In the first part of your paper, you pose your research question and describe it in the context of the existing literature. You also discuss the significance or importance of your question. Here you are answering the "so what?" question. So what if you answer this question? What does it matter to you or anyone else? What is the theoretical or practical significance of the question?

In the second part, you present the data you have collected. For example, if your question was about the influence of personal and environmental factors on self-injury in jails and lockups, you would review the studies that have been done in the area. You will find that constructing a chart that summarizes all the studies is very helpful in reviewing and synthesizing a large number of studies. In our example, we are dealing with the findings of empirical studies. Charts are equally useful for organizing arguments and perspectives when your research question has to do with U.S. foreign policy in the Middle East, for example.

The final major part of your paper is the conclusion. Here, you weigh the evidence, interpret the results, and draw a conclusion. This is the most difficult and the most rewarding part of the paper. The empirical findings and expert opinions on just about everything you can imagine are equivocal. No matter what you study you will find mixed results. It is your job to evaluate and interpret these results and answer the question you posed. Often your answer will include additional questions and a call for more research and thinking on the subject.

You should take care to use proper grammar and style in the final version of your paper. The rules of grammar and style help you to communicate clearly and effectively. An indispensable and accessible source on style and grammar is William Strunk and E. B. White's *The Elements of Style*.

A paper assignment gives you the opportunity to demonstrate your ability to conduct library research, integrate material from a variety of sources, apply what you have gleaned from lectures and assigned readings, and write a clear, organized, well-documented paper. If you don't give yourself adequate time, you will not adequately demonstrate your abilities in any of these areas. One characteristic of the hastily done paper is that it takes the form of a chronology of what the student has read. The student merely describes the contents of each article in the sequence in which they were read without attempting to integrate or synthesize the material. This kind of paper will surely get you a low grade from any honest and competent professor.

There are many different kinds of papers or approaches to writing a paper. Most good professors will provide you with specifics about the form of the paper when they make the assignment. If your professor doesn't, ask him or her to specify a form or approach. Also ask the professor if he or she is willing to review a draft of the paper for you before the final due date. A review before the final draft can go a long way in improving the paper and your grade.

If your professor doesn't provide you with a model or approach, you can use one of the four described here, if appropriate for the topic. The following models were developed for a course that focused on a social problem.

Specific Research Question Approach

This is the model that has been used so far in this book in discussing paper writing. In this approach, you derive a specific research question from your reading or the lectures. Your paper is driven by the question, and your purpose is to answer that question. How you phrase the question, is very important. For example, "Why do they do it?" and "Why don't we do it?" are questions that can take you in very different directions.

1. Introduction
   A. Statement of the Research Question
   B. Significance or Importance of the Question
      Why are you asking the question? So what if you answer it?
   C. Synopsis or Map of the Structure of the Paper
      Prepare the reader for what is in store.

2. Presentation and Evaluation of the Evidence
   Review and assess the evidence (expert opinion, research, and conceptual or theoretical) relevant to your question. Discuss the strengths and weaknesses of the evidence.

3. Conclusion
   A. Best Answer to the Question
   B. Additional Questions
      Discuss the questions that emerge from your investigation of the research question. Suggest strategies for obtaining the information needed to answer these questions.

General Approach

For some papers, you are not expected to develop a specific research question. The purpose of the paper is to introduce you to the literature on a fairly broad topic, and your paper should reflect your reading. Here your purpose is not to answer a specific question. It is to describe broadly what is known about a phenomenon by integrating what you have read about it in several sources. For example, instead of requiring you to answer a question about the contribution of personal and environment factors to self-destructive behavior in a specific institution, some professors would require that you write a paper on a broad topic like suicide in American society or teen suicide.

Presented below is a suggested structure for this kind of paper. This is only a suggestion. The actual structure of the paper will vary by topic and individual style.

1. Introduction

   Establish the significance of the topic you have selected, and give the reader a map of what is in the body of the paper. Tell the reader what to expect. Prepare the reader's mind for what is to come. Give a synopsis of the structure of the paper.

2. Explanation of Nature and Extent of the Problem
   A. Estimates of Extent and Cost

   Provide empirical research findings and expert opinion estimates of the prevalence and cost of the phenomenon. Assess the methodological soundness of the estimates. If you do not find any estimates, indicate where you looked for them. Be specific. If you find three or more estimates, construct a chart to present them in addition to describing them in the body of your paper.

   B. Nature
   1) Shape

   Describe the shapes of the phenomenon. What forms does it take?

   2) Correlates and Conditions

   What personal and situational characteristics are associated with the phenomenon? Who is involved? What are the situational factors that are associated with the phenomenon? Is there a typical sequence of steps involved? Are there environmental correlates?

3. Explanations

   What explanations have been offered in the literature for the phenomenon? Are these explanations based on empirical evidence?

This section of the paper will overlap to some extent with section 2.B.2 of the paper in that it may be appropriate to offer plausible explanations of the associations reported in that section or the associations or sequences described may suggest plausible explanations.

4. Conclusion
A. Implications
What are the implications of what you have discovered about this kind of phenomenon for dealing with it? What are the implications for the future?
B. Questions
What questions that require answers have emerged from your investigation of this kind of phenomenon?

Research Proposal Approach

In this approach, you develop a research design to collect the information needed to answer a question you pose. Any topic that is appropriate for the specific research question approach is also appropriate for the research proposal approach. The difference is that in the former you are using other people's evidence to draw a conclusion whereas in the latter you are collecting your own.

It is not a good idea to take this approach unless you have taken a research methods course.

1. Statement of the Problem
This includes your research question and the source and importance of the question.

2. Methods
Present the modes of observation or techniques that you are going to use to collect your information. You must discuss why you selected these methods rather than alternatives, and you must address the reliability and validity of your methods.

3. Sampling
   Include a description of your sampling design, including a discussion of representativeness, efficiency, and size.

4. Analysis
   What techniques do you intend to use to analyze the data?

5. Expected Findings

Issues Approach

The issues approach consists of a discussion of the legal, moral, ethical, and operational issues surrounding a policy, intervention, or program. It is important in writing an issues paper not to present uninformed opinions. Your conclusions should be based on empirical research, logical deduction, and/or principled arguments. Examples of topics that are appropriate for an issues paper are "Right to Life: Does an Adult Have the Right to End His Own Life?" and "Who's Responsible: What Is the Responsibility of a College When a Student Commits Suicide?"

1. Introduction
   A. Statement of the Central Issue and Its Importance
   B. Related Issues
   C. Synopsis of the Structure of the Paper
2. Discussion
   This should be an informed discussion of positions on the issue. You should outline the shape of current debates on the issues and define and discuss the dimensions of importance.
3. Conclusion
   State your position on the issue, and defend your position.

Documentation

Before we leave the topic of writing a research paper and go on to taking examinations, a few points on documentation are in order. The first point is to make sure that you give proper recognition to the words and ideas of others. If you do not, you are intellectually dishonest, and you have committed plagiarism. You have taken the work of others and presented it as your own. It is very serious business, and it can get you expelled from school.

There are several styles of documentation. In many cases, your professor will recommend one. If he or she does not, I recommend the American Psychological Association (APA) style. In my experience, it is by far the easiest and most sensible system, and it is appropriate for all subjects and disciplines. The latest edition of the *Publication Manual of the American Psychological Association* will provide you with all the information you need for using this system.

Testing

The best advice for taking examinations in college is to review and anticipate. For major examinations, such as midterms and finals, you should begin your review at least a week in advance of the examination. You should divide your total review time into several sessions that cover distinct segments of the material. You should schedule your review time for a specific examination well in advance to make sure that (1) you do not completely disrupt your daily patterns of eating, sleeping, working, and recreating; and (2) the review does not interfere with your regular school work or reviewing for other tests during examination week.

The worst thing you can do is not review at all. The second worst thing you can do is to cram. Although cramming may benefit short-term memory, the anxiety it engenders may offset these gains.

In reviewing, you should anticipate questions that will be asked on the exam. You don't have to be an oracle to do this. It is actually quite simple.

Despite the popular myth, most professors do not

spend hours poring over the footnotes in assigned readings looking for obscure points to work into test items or questions. Most professors try to construct tests that have content validity. This means that they ask questions or develop items that adequately represent the content of the course. Happily, the content of the course should also be adequately represented in your notes on readings and lectures.

Attending most classes is important, but attending the class before a test is crucial. The custom is that the last class or so before a major test, the professor will tell you explicitly whether there is any special emphasis on specific course content (certain topics or certain sources of content, such as lectures or readings) and what the format of the test will be (essay, objective, problem-solving, or some combination). If it is an objective test, the professor might even tell you the specific format it will take, for example, true-false, matching, short answer, traditional multiple choice, or application of principles.

No matter what the format of the exam, the questions usually will be derived from the main body of ideas around which the course is structured. Since these very ideas form the main body of your notes on lectures and readings, it is possible to conduct a comprehensive review just using your notes.

The procedure is to make a question out of each major item in your notes. Simply answer each question. Reread pertinent sections of the text when you cannot answer a question satisfactorily.

According to Robinson, simple essay questions will be sufficient for your comprehensive review. You do not have to bother to try to fit questions into the exact format the exam should take, such as matching or multiple choice. It will slow you down and result in a less comprehensive review. If you know the format of the exam, however, you should practice answering a few questions in that format. If possible, practice by using an old examination.

If you decide to reread as your method of review, make sure that you do it with exam questions in mind. One way to reduce the amount you reread is to turn the headings in your books and notes into exam questions, and read only to verify the correctness of your answers or to find an answer when you cannot answer a question.

Just about everybody suffers from at least mild test anxiety. It is the first thing you have to deal with when you enter an examination room. Sometimes it can begin long before the examination and interfere with how effectively you study. In a small proportion of cases, students become immobilized by anxiety, and they cannot study at all.

Test anxiety was discussed earlier in relation to the anxiety gumption trap. Here, the main points of the discussion will be recapitulated. If you are prone to test anxiety, you should carefully reread the "Anxiety" section in Part Three of this book.

As you will recall, anxiety, like most other problems, is a product of time-place dissonance. The problem stems from worrying about the future consequences of the task you are doing in the present. The way to end anxiety is simply to let go of the future and concentrate on what you are doing in the present. This, of course, is easier said than done. But there are techniques that can help to alleviate and control anxiety.

Anxiety, like other emotions, has cognitive, physiological, and behavioral components. The cognitive component is worry. The best way to deal with worry is to let it go and concentrate on the task at hand—that is, studying or taking the test. Try the "bagging" technique that was described in Part Three. Allow yourself time to worry at the end of the study session or test, and bag it until then. Often you will find that if you can successfully deal with the cognitive component of worry, physiological symptoms will diminish or disappear.

The physiological symptoms of worry are increased autonomic nervous system activity that results in a general feeling of tension. Deep breathing exercises, like the cleansing breath described in Part Three, can help relieve the tension and produce a sense of calmness. These exercises are especially helpful right before the examination and when you feel tense during the examination.

If you take care of the cognitive and physiological aspects of anxiety, the anxiety-related behavioral problems, for example, poor performance, will not be an issue. There are some behaviors or activities that can promote test anxiety, and you should, of course, avoid them.

One activity that is notorious for spiking test anxiety is discussing the test with a group of peers right before the examination. Test manuals invariably tell you to avoid this situation. There is absolutely nothing to recommend chatting about the exam minutes before you open your blue book. Take this time to compose yourself. Count a few breaths in your seat or do some kinhin. If you have to talk to avoid being rude, keep it light.

Once you have the exam, the first thing you do is carefully read the instructions. This is not always easy. You're anxious to see what the questions look like and to get on with the exam. Hold back. Relax. Read the instructions with right effort. You might even try reciting the instructions to yourself in your own words. It will only take a minute. It might be well worth the time. Instructions, especially those for essay exams, can contain crucial information, such as how many questions to answer. Keep in mind that your ability to follow instructions is the first skill measured by any test.

If the exam is an objective test, start answering the questions in sequence. Answer the questions about which you are confident, and return to answer the questions that are more difficult for you. If there is no penalty for wrong answers, take a guess rather than leaving a blank.

For essay examinations, carefully read through the entire examination before you begin. Take note of the proportion of total points allocated to each question. It tells you how much time you should devote to each answer. If you are given a choice, take a few minutes to think carefully about which questions you should answer.

Start by answering the easiest question. Reread the question carefully, and answer the question that is asked. If you are asked to list reasons, list reasons. If you are asked to compare and contrast alternatives, compare and contrast alternatives. If you are asked to discuss consequences, discuss consequences, do not discuss causes. I have read dozens of student examinations that featured very good answers to questions that were not asked.

Once you are sure what the question is asking, make a list of the key points that should be covered in your answer, and use your list to develop an outline. Your outline should present the points to be covered in some sensible sequence. Your answer will consist of elaborating on these points to demonstrate that you have a firm grasp of important concepts and central ideas. Avoid padding at all cost. Make sure that everything you write is pertinent. Including superfluous information to increase the bulk of your answer is a good way to move your grade in the direction of a goose egg.

Legibility counts. There are few things more irritating to a professor than trying to decipher poor penmanship. Some research evidence suggests that illegible handwriting can cost you a letter grade on an essay examination.

In the unhappy event that you run out of time before you can answer all the questions on an essay exam, write a short note to the professor explaining that you ran out of time, and write an outline for the answer for each question that you do not have time to answer with a complete essay. Dr. Gordon Green, author of *Getting Straight A's*, suggests that you can often salvage most of the credit assigned to a question by supplying a good outline.

Listening

There is some research evidence that knowing how to listen in class is a more important academic skill than knowing how to read a textbook. The first step in becoming a good listener is to make it to class. The next step is to find a good seat, that is, one in the front or middle rows. Don't let your ego keep you in the back of the classroom because you think you're either too cool, too dumb, or too shy. If you sit in the front there are fewer distractions, and it is easier to give your complete attention to the lecture or discussion. Seating position and attendance are too important to allow ego or anxiety dictate. Both have been found to be positively associated with performance in college.

The third step in good listening is always to come to class prepared. Read assigned readings before class. It will usually make the lecture much more comprehensible to you, and it will allow you to participate fully in discussions. Once again, don't let ego get in your way. If what life brings you in the moment is a class discussion, participate with right effort.

When you go to a lecture, you should enter with an open mind, a beginner's mind. While in the lecture hall, be only in the lecture hall. Become totally absorbed in what the professor is saying. At that moment there is only the lecture; give it your total attention. Follow the advice of Harada-roshi as told to Peter Matthiessen by Glassman-sensei: "... when you go to teisho [a lecture], you should be the only listener in the room. If there is just you and the teacher, you will listen: otherwise, you tend to give responsibility to others." This is wonderful advice. Listen as if you are the only one at the lecture. It is so simple.

You should take notes when you listen to a lecture. Contrary to popular belief, note-taking does not interfere with listening. Note-taking does provide you with a written record of the material presented in class, and if you use your notes correctly, your information loss over time will be minimized.

One popular method for taking class notes is called the Cornell system. According to Pauk, it consists of three steps.

Step 1. Preparation

Obtain a large loose-leaf notebook, and draw a line the length of the page about two and one-half inches from the left margin. A large notebook will provide you with plenty of space for taking notes, and the loose-leaf feature will allow you to insert handouts and reorganize pages. Drawing the line will divide each page into space to the right of the line for taking notes in class and space to the left of the line, called the recall column, for recording headings and brief notes after class.

Step 2. Lecture Notes

Take simple, clear notes in paragraph form. Do not try to structure your notes in terms of some fancy outline. Just get down the main ideas in a form that will make sense when you review your notes. Don't skimp on space. Leave plenty of space between central ideas, concepts, and points. Link supporting information, secondary concepts, and important examples and illustrations to the central ideas by using letters, numbers, indentations, and/or arrows. Do not try to write down all the details, especially of illustrative material. Try to capture the general flow of an argument or development of an idea.

Step 3. After the Lecture

Review your notes as soon after the lecture as you can. Identify missing and ambiguous information, and make plans to gather the information you need to make additions and correction. If you have your textbook or a friend's notes handy, you can do a lot of it on the spot. Otherwise, bring a reasonable list of questions to ask the professor in the next class. If you have taken pretty good notes, the work at this stage should be minimal.

As you review your notes, underline or in some way indicate words and phrases that represent key concepts and ideas. After you have done this, review your notes again. But this time use the recall column, the two and one-half-inch left column on each page that you created by drawing a vertical line. Use the recall column to record key words and phrases that represent the content of your notes, which appear to the immediate right of the recall column. One benefit of developing and selecting key words and phrases is that it requires that you think about the material in the notes and organize it in some fashion. This helps with both understanding and recall.

Recitation should be your next task. Cover your lecture notes on the right side, and recite in your own words the facts, ideas, and arguments associated with each of the key words and phrases appearing in your recall column. After your recitation for each key word, uncover and examine your notes to test your accuracy.

Scheduling

The importance of planning and the benefits of using a daily schedule were discussed in relation to the impatience gumption trap, in Part Three. There it was stressed that planning for the major tasks to be accomplished in a semester and developing daily schedules that reflect your semester plan can go a long way in reducing anxiety on a daily and semester level.

If you plan ahead and complete your schoolwork in manageable daily increments, you will avoid the devasting experience of trying to do everything at the end of the semester. Leaving everything until the end never works. It drains all your gumption and leaves you tense and exhausted. In addition, if you wait until the last minute to do your work, you never develop effective study skills through self-examination and practice.

Planning is easy. Simply write on a calendar the dates of major events, such as examinations and key assignments. Then write in the dates on which you should have important subcomponents of the task completed in order to be ready on the day of the major event. For example, a research paper requires that you specify dates when you will (1) finish the preliminary reading, (2) select a topic, (3) pose a research question, (4) complete the research, (5) finish writing certain sections, (6) finish the first draft, (6) edit the first draft, (7) produce the final copy for submission, and (8) submit the paper. If you set these dates and estimate how much time each subcomponent will require, you are in a position to include part of a subcomponent into your daily schedule.

In your daily schedule, you should allocate time for (1) routine activities, such as recreation, meditation, eating, sleeping, letter-writing, and working at your job; (2) daily assignments, such as reading and writing assignments for class (homework); and (3) major events or central assignments, such as examinations and papers. The exact form your daily schedule takes is a matter of personal choice. Some people require a fairly detailed schedule with tasks broken down into activities. Others merely need to list in some sensible order what they have to accomplish on a certain day. The important thing is to have a schedule, and to stick by it as best you can.

How much time should you allocate to studying? The standard is to schedule two hours of work outside class for each hour you spend in class. This means that for a three-credit-hour course, you should study six hours per week. If you are taking a fifteen-hour course load, you should be putting in thirty hours a week dancing with your books. The amount of time you put into different courses, of course, will vary. Some courses require more time than others, and some people possess more effective study skills than others. Keep in mind that how effectively you study is more important than how long you study. If you work with right effort and proper technique for one hour, you will accomplish more than if you just go through the motions for a much longer time.

It is important to build in breaks when studying. After you complete each half-hour or so of study, do a little stretching or a few cleansing breaths. Take a few minutes off when you switch from one topic or task to another. End each break with a renewed commitment to study with right effort.

Part Five

END AND BEGINNING

Studying with Right Effort: A Review

Dancing with your books, or studying with right effort, total concentration, or complete involvement merely requires that you sweep your mind clean of impediments so your mind's light can shine naturally and exclusively on the task at hand. Achieving this state of effortless effort or flow, however, is easier said than done. It requires patience and practice.

The steps, suggestions, reminders, and pointers listed in this section are intended to help you study with right effort. After you have practiced studying with right effort for a while, you can develop your own list that is uniquely suited to you. In the meantime, try the following list for starters.

1. Clear your mind by doing zazen, kinhin, or cleansing breaths for a few minutes.
2. Feel your mind relax. Feel your mind open. Prepare your mind to accept whatever lessons you are about to learn or whatever schoolwork you are about to do.
3. Find your beginner's mind. Prepare yourself to go on a journey to a place you have never been where you will learn something new and valuable. Forget about the destination. Concentrate on the trip itself. Don't worry about goals and results. Focus on process.
4. Make an explicit commitment to yourself to study with right effort for a set amount of time or until you finish certain tasks. Promise yourself that you

will focus exclusively on studying and you will let go of other times, places, and tasks. Convince yourself that the only proper thing to do in the allotted time is to study. Don't give yourself the choice of doing anything else.

5. Accept that you have to be where you are doing what you are doing. Right now there is no place else you can be other than where you are.

6. Settle into doing what you are doing. Invest yourself in each moment. Sink into your books. Absorb and be absorbed by the task at hand. Embrace your books and dance.

7. Stay centered in the moment and the task at hand. When you notice that your thoughts are straying from your books to other times and places, let go, and recenter.

8. Let go of self. There is no separate self and task or person-task distinction. You and your books are inseparably melded in the task of the moment. Thoughts of a separate you studying your books only get in the way of studying.

9. When irrelevant thoughts enter your mind, let them go. Recognize them for what they are, witness them, and then refocus on the task at hand. Don't cling to thoughts, don't chase after them, don't attach to them. Don't give them the power to take you away from your books. Let them vanish into thin air.

10. Study as if it's the only reason you were put on this earth. Just study. Now!

Techniques and Exercises: A Summary and Index

Techniques and exercises designed to promote right effort and deal with impediments to flow have been presented throughout this book. Here is a handy directory to these techniques and exercises.

Technique	Problem Addressed	Location
Zazen	Any impediment to right effort	pp. 54–63
Mind-as-light visualization	Loss of focus	pp. 75–76
Center-of-wheel visualization	Loss of focus	p. 76
Dropping "I"	Ego	pp. 88–91
Kinhin	Test anxiety	p. 96
Cleansing breath	Test anxiety	p. 96
One step at a time	Initial anxiety or beginner's anxiety	pp. 99–100
Energy breathing	Loss of energy or interest	pp. 103–105
Expansion	Any impediment to right effort	pp. 108–111
Bagging	Worry and anxiety	pp. 112–113
Rainbow light relaxation	Tension	pp. 114–116

After you have been trying to study with right effort for a while, you should conduct a self-assessment to determine which particular impediment interferes most with your application of right effort to your schoolwork. You should include as part of your daily routine the technique or techniques that address your particular set of problems.

Sticking to a daily routine is not easy. At one time or another, you will fall into the progress trap. There will be doubt, and you will question the purpose of what you are doing. There may be some backsliding where you miss days of following your routine. You will tend to slide back to your old ways when you are under a lot of pressure or no pressure at all.

During these times, when it seems that your routine to promote right effort is not working or is not needed, it is especially important to follow your routine. It will go a long way in strengthening your commitment to right effort if you get through the hard times with right effort. At some point, you will realize that with right effort hard times and easy times do not matter. The only thing that matters is full absorption in the moment, whatever that moment may bring. All you have to do to reach this state of perfect momentariness is begin and continue. Dance that first step with your books, and keep those feet moving.

Conclusion

Dainin Katagiri, abbot of the Minnesota Zen Meditation Center, tells his students, "If you sit zazen, zazen is your life, whether you like it or not. When you study literature, literature is life itself. When you study science, science must be burning the flame of life." This simple message is the central point of this book. The only advice offered is that when you study, just study. Everything else written between these two covers is intended to help you to put this simple advice into practice—an immensely difficult task.

Much of what has been written in this book has been drawn from the popular literature on Zen. However, this book should not be considered a book about Zen. It merely borrows some ideas that have been expressed in relation to Zen and applies them to studying and learning.

The purpose of Zen is to penetrate and return to the core of existence or origin where everything resides in a perfect state of suchness or oneness. Here is the seat of Zen enlightenment, which cannot be described. It can only be experienced.

Although the Zen realization, intuition, or experience that your deepest nature is one and the same as that of the whole universe cannot be expressed in concepts or language, there are a number of books that do a fine job in describing Zen practices and insights as well as they can be expressed in words. I have listed below some of my favorites.

The Three Pillars of Zen, by Philip Kapleau. This book is a compendium of information about the actual practice of Zen. The author, Roshi Philip Kapleau of the Zen Center of Rochester, New York, includes a great deal of the kind of verbatim dialogue between teacher and students that you will not find in other sources. The lectures by Yasutani-Roshi included in this volume are invaluable to the beginning student.

Taking the Path of Zen, by Robert Aitken. Like Philip Kapleau, Robert Aitken, who is also an American Zen Roshi, has written a very practical guide to the practice of Zen. He provides the reader with a sense of what it is like to practice at a Zen center, and he furnishes clear instructions on the practice of zazen.

Nine-Headed Dragon River, by Peter Matthiessen. This is a powerfully and beautifully written book by the award-winning author of *The Snow Leopard.* In this work, Peter Matthiessen takes us on his personal Zen journey. We travel with him from his inauspicious introduction to Zen on Long Island to his tour of Japanese Zen monasteries with his sensei, Bernard Glassman. In between, we experience the highs and lows of Zen training and get a lesson in the history of Zen.

Zen Mind, Beginner's Mind, by Shunryu Suzuki. This is a gentle and charming collection of talks by a Zen master. Most of the material in this book is accessible to students without previous knowledge of Zen, and the book is very useful to those who have been practicing for a while. Other books of talks by Zen teachers that are useful to those who already have some knowledge of Zen are *Mountain Record of Zen Talks,* by John Loori, and *Returning to Silence: Zen Practice in Daily Life,* by Dainin Katagiri.

Zen and the Birds of Appetite, by Thomas Merton. This collection of essays by the well-known author and monk discusses Zen in a Western context. It contains an exchange between Father Merton and D. T.

Suzuki, the man who is credited with popularizing Zen in America. The material in the book is well presented and compelling, but it is not for everyone. Only those with a philosophical/theological bent should read it.

The Supreme Doctrine: Psychological Encounters in Zen Thought, by Hubert Benoit. In this work, which features a foreword by Aldous Huxley, Dr. Hubert Benoit discusses Western psychological thought and psychiatric practice in relation to Zen principles. It is not light reading. It is fascinating reading.

If you want additional information about Zen, go to a Zen center, and jump in with both feet. Many centers offer one-day workshops on Zen philosophy and meditation and weekend or week-long meditation retreats.

BIBLIOGRAPHY

Aitken, Robert. 1982. *Taking the Path of Zen*. San Francisco: North Point.

Allport, Gordon W. 1960. *Personality and Social Encounter*. Boston: Beacon.

Becker, Howard S. 1986. *Writing for Social Scientist: How to Start and Finish Your Thesis, Book or Article*. Chicago: University of Chicago Press.

Benoit, Hubert. 1955. *The Supreme Doctrine: Psychological Encounters in Zen Thought*. New York: Inner Traditions International.

Berger, K. T. 1988. *Zen Driving*. New York: Ballantine.

Blackburn, Dan, and Jorgenson, Maryann. 1976. *Zen and the Cross Country Skier*. Pasadena, CA: Ward Ritchie.

Bradon, David. 1976. *Zen in the Art of Helping*. New York: Dell.

Deshimura, Taisen. 1982. *The Zen Way to the Martial Arts*, trans. N. Amphoux. New York: E. P. Dutton

Endler, Norman. 1980. "Person-situation Interaction and Anxiety," *Handbook on Anxiety and Stress*, I. Dutach, L. Schlesinger, and associates, eds. Pp. 249–266. Washington: Jossey-Boss.

Fromm, Eric, Suzuki, Daisetz Teitaro, and DeMartino, Richard. 1960. *Zen Buddhism and Psychoanalysis*. New York: Harper and Row.

Goldberg, Natalie. 1986. *Writing Down the Bones: Freeing the Writer Within*. Boston: Shambhala.

Goleman, Daniel. 1986. "Concentration Is Linked to Euphoric States of Mind." *New York Times,* 4 March.

Green, Gordon W., Jr. 1985. *Getting Straight A's.* Secaucus, NJ: Lyle Stuart.

Humphreys, Christmas. 1962. *Zen: A Way of Life.* Boston: Little, Brown.

———.1971. *A Western Approach to Zen.* Wheaton, IL: The Theosophical Publishing House.

———.1974. *Exploring Buddhism.* Wheaton, IL: The Theosophical Publishing House.

Hyams, Joe. 1979. *Zen in the Martial Arts.* Los Angeles: J. P. Tarcher.

Izutsu, Toshihiko. 1977. *Toward a Philosophy of Zen Buddhism.* Boulder: Prajna.

Kapleau, Philip, ed. 1980. *The Three Pillars of Zen.* Rev. ed. Garden City, NY: Anchor.

Kasulis, T. P. 1981. *Zen Action Zen Person.* Honolulu: The University Press of Hawaii.

Katagiri, Cainin. 1988. *Returning to Silence: Zen Practice in Daily Life.* Boston: Shambhala.

LeShan, Lawrence. 1974. *How to Meditate.* New York: Bantam.

Levey, Joel. 1987. *The Fine Arts of Relaxation, Concentration, and Meditation: Ancient Skills for Modern Minds.* London: Wisdom.

Levine, Donald N. 1984. "The Liberal Arts and the Martial Arts." *Liberal Education,* Vol. LXX, pp. 235–251.

Linssen, Robert. 1969. *Zen: The Art of Life.* New York: Pyramid Communications.

Loori, John Daido. 1988. *Mountain Record of Zen Talks.* Boston: Shambhala.

Low, Albert. 1976. *Zen and Creative Management.* Garden City, NY: Anchor.

Lozoff, Bo. 1985. *We're All Doing Time*. Durham, NC: Hanuman Foundation.

Maezumi, Hakuyu Taizmo, and Glassman, Bernard Tetsugen. 1978. *The Hazy Moon of Enlightenment*. Los Angeles: Center Publications.

Matthiessen, Peter. *The Snow Leopard*. New York: Viking Penguin.

————. 1985. Nine-Headed Dragon River. Boston: Shambhala.

Memering, Dean. 1983. *Research Writing: A Complete Guide to Research Papers*. Englewood Cliffs, NJ: Prentice-Hall.

Merton, Thomas. 1968. *Zen and the Birds of Appetite*. New York: New Directions.

Nieves, Luis R. 1984. *Coping in College*. Princeton, NJ: Educational Testing Service.

Park, Sung Bae. 1983. *Buddhist Faith and Sudden Enlightenment*. Albany, NY: State University of New York Press.

Pauk, Walter. 1974. *How to Study*. Boston: Houghton Mifflin.

Pirsig, Robert M. 1974. *Zen and the Art of Motorcycle Maintenance*. New York: Bantam.

Reynolds, David K. 1984. *Playing Ball on Running Water*. New York: Quill.

Robinson, Francis. 1970. *Effective Study*. 4th ed. New York: Harper and Row.

Rohé, Fred. 1974. *The Zen of Running*. New York: Random House.

Schon, Donald A. 1963. *Displacement of Concepts*. London: Tavistock.

Suzuki, Shunryu. 1970. *Zen Mind, Beginner's Mind*. New York: Weatherhill.

Tendzin, Ösel. 1982. *Buddha in the Palm of Your Hand*. Boulder: Shambhala.

Trout, Kilgore. 1974. *Venus on the Half-shell*. New York: Dell.

INDEX